DIAMONDS IN THE ROUGH

Hidden Treasures of P.T.L.

Written and Compiled by
Ray Walters

Edited by
Linda Tomblin

Copyright 1998 by Ray Walters. All rights reserved. Printed in the United States of America. No part of this book may be used or reproduced in any manner whatsoever without written permission of the author except in the case of brief quotations.

For further information or speaking engagements, contact Ray Walters, 423 Sweet Gum Drive, Fort Mill, S.C. 29715 (803-548-7718).

FIRST EDITION

Scripture verses are taken from the King James version of the Bible.

ISBN 0-939241-30-7

Walters, Ray

The author of this book, Ray Walters, has compiled this volume with permission from actual letters and interviews with subjects. Because of space availability, he was not able to use all letters or photographs received and some have been shortened. Any letter which was not used is being considered for use in his second book, "More Diamonds In The Rough."

Editing and layout of book by Linda Tomblin, a private publishing consultant, who acts as an editor only and assumes no responsibility for the content and/or accuracy of any statement herein.

Contents

Chapter 1
GOD'S GLOW 1

Chapter 2
GLORIOUS GEMS 7

Chapter 3
PRECIOUS PRAYER 37

Chapter 4
RADIATING RICHES 53

Chapter 5
GOLDEN GLITTERS 75

Chapter 6
SPLENDID SERVANTHOOD 81

Chapter 7
WINNING WEALTH 87

Chapter 8
GLEAMING GIFTS 99

Chapter 9
JOYFUL JEWELS 111

Chapter 10
MAGNIFICENT MINERS 121

Chapter 11
　　FABULOUS FINDS 137

Chapter 12
　　PRICELESS PROMISES 153

Chapter 13
　　RARE RICHES 163

Chapter 14
　　REMEMBRANCE RING 201

Chapter 15
　　TOMORROW'S TREASURES 247

Foreword
By Linda Tomblin

These are the unheralded stories of God's *"Diamonds in the Rough,"* . . . the men, women and children who came through the gates of P.T.L. . . . were touched by God, and returned home to change their world. Many of these people arrived saddened, troubled, defeated, searching for answers . . . and left with a renewed confidence in God, joyful reassurance, and revelations for their lives.

Today the doors to P.T.L. have closed, but the doorway to God has been magnified because of these individuals' open arms and loving hearts. Many new ministries have originated as a result of these people being called by God to come to this specific place for His specific purpose . . . and then being commissioned by Him to go back to their churches, businesses and communities.

Ray Walters and I realize that we have only uncovered small portions of these treasures. There are still thousands of stories hidden out there waiting to be mined. By sharing these testimonies, letters, and interviews, we hope you will be able to see the expansion and extension of God's love and mercy through these servants of God. Many are still working with outreach programs that they helped to found. Others are busy in their churches as laymen and women. Still others simply went home to quietly become a better Christian mother, father, husband, wife, child, neighbor, or friend.

Three qualities tie all these people together. First, they are Christian workers. Second, they are performing their work gently and privately without seeking publicity or praise. And third, God's love and grace are being multiplied countless times over through these individuals.

They came. They saw God's love. And because of their personal experience, God is living today in the hearts of other people. And other people . . . and other people. It goes on and on and on . . . through "People That Love."

Ray Walters

Dedication

I want to dedicate this book first to God and His glory and honor, and then to my wonderful wife Margia and precious daughter RaLynn, both of whom have worked with me and been lovingly patient with the time it has taken me to accomplish this task.

Acknowledgements

A special thank you to Myra Bumgardner for the inspiring painting she created for the cover, and for giving us permission to use her poems and beautiful letter in the book. (If you have a need for her artistic talents, or if you'd just like to see more of her work, visit her web site at http.//www.inspirationalart.com or call her at 1-888-630-9156.) Myra is best known for her painting "Jesus Is Coming Again."

Thank you to Reverend Rex E. Faile, Sr. for allowing us to use his poem "A Diamond In The Rough." I am grateful to God that He allowed Pastor Faile to write this poem and then "happen" to meet Margia and learn about the book. God's timing excited all of us!

Thank you to Florence W. Biros and Dr. John W. Lovitt for their kindness in giving their endorsement to this project. I appreciate their thoughtful comments.

Thank you to Linda Tomblin, my editor, in her untiring efforts to make this the type of book God would have it to be. I would recommend her highly to anyone who wants to have the fun and pleasure of writing a book of their own. (You can reach her at P.O. Box 404, Spindale, N.C. or 704-286-1953.)

Thank you most of all to our Heavenly Father for giving

me the vision for this book and for the wonderful people who have contributed their stories and letters . . . letters which indicate that not one of these people came for the "glitter" of P.T.L. They came, . . . they came back . . . and they stayed because of the Spirit of the Lord which entered their hearts in the love and help that was given them and the opportunities that they had to give back in ministry to others.

And last, thank you, Dear Reader, for taking the time to read and prayerfully consider the messages in this book. May the clouds of darkness which have hovered over this land, disappear in the brightness of God's glory!

A Message From Ray Walters

Several words typically come to mind when one hears the mention of P.T.L. -- lies, deceit, wealth, greediness, trial, exploitation, prison . . . . All of those words and more sound familiar to most of us, but sometimes we forget that there are always two sides. Have you heard the other words that describe P.T.L. . . . words such as love, beauty, friendship, devotion, dedication, and encouragement? Has anyone told you of the beauty of God's presence in the early days at P.T.L.? Do you know about the love that existed and still exists between the people? Have you any idea of the numbers of people who were touched by God and went away to serve Him?

As owner of Noah's Toy Shoppe, I was present to hear the prayers prayed by the shop owners on Main Street. I was there to see the way the visitors ministered to each other. I lived in this place where foul language and smoking weren't allowed . . . a safe place where children could be turned loose to play . . . a place where a wonderful man called "Uncle Henry" loved everyone with an obvious love.

For a moment, I'd like for you to imagine, if you will, strolling through the grounds of Heritage Village in Fort Mill, South Carolina, with me. A cool breeze softens the touch of the warm southern sun on our faces as we enter mines where treasures are hidden. Some of them have names which are familiar to us: workshops, seminars, healing sessions, Bible studies. Other names, less familiar but equally intriguing, are the Upper Room, Fort Hope, C.O.P.E., the Tender Loving Care Adoption Agency, and Freedom Ministries. Perhaps we will be like other visitors who came to this place with problems and heartaches . . . and left with treasures. I have a feeling, through this book, that we will carry bags full of diamonds away. I can say this with confidence because the greatest jewels of P.T.L. were not jewels of financial worth, not gold faucets and gaudy bracelets, but jewels of spiritual value.

Diamonds in the Rough is compiled of actual letters from people all over the United States who were touched by P.T.L. They are written by the people — to you, the reader. These letters cover what happened for, with, and through them at Heritage U.S.A. and what is going on in their lives today as a result of the hidden treasures that they mined at P.T.L. The purpose of this book is to bring to light the many good stories . . . the stories that have been overlooked and overpowered by the media hype surrounding the scandal.

These are the true, untold stories of individuals, testimonies in the words of those who were touched by . . . or who touched someone . . . through the various avenues of P.T.L. This book is being written because we believe people today are ready to examine the "whole" truth . . . ready to see the "good." *Diamonds in the Rough* will help readers do that. As author of this book, I am able to give an "inside view" of P.T.L. and Heritage USA. I know the people and have been able to obtain the necessary interviews and letters. Although my family and I were close friends with the Bakkers, I neither condemn nor give my stamp of approval to the controversial happenings. I am more interested in telling the stories of the people whose lives were turned around. I simply want to "share the good news." Without P.T.L. and the ministries that evolved, the following stories would never have taken place. My prayer is that you will sit down alone and read these letters carefully and prayerfully. Allow your mind and heart to enfold the words. These people speak for themselves.

This project began when I started to write my life story, at age 82. We were living in San Antonio, and since we had a large family and there were many interruptions, my wife Margia and I decided that I needed to take a sabbatical leave. So I moved to Belmont, North Carolina, to write the book. Alone in my one bedroom apartment, I began writing, and it was amazing how things came so clearly to mind.

It was great fun until I got to the part about my involvement with P.T.L. I knew it needed to be told, but each time I tried to write about it, nothing seemed to go right. I simply couldn't do it. I couldn't imagine what was wrong. After all, as owner and operator of Noah's Toy Shoppe, I knew more than most about both the good times and the bad at P.T.L. Finally I asked, "Lord, what is the matter? Why can't I write about this?"

And it seemed like a voice said, "What about me? Where do I come into your story?" Suddenly I realized that there had been many bad things written about P.T.L. in the last several years, but nothing had been written about the good parts. In a few days, I knew without a doubt what I had to do. I had to bring to light the good things that had happened at P.T.L. -- the good things that were still happening. Ever since that time, I've had goose bumps on my arms. I've never had more fun in my life as I follow God's directions to uncover and write about *Diamonds in the Rough, Hidden Treasures of P.T.L.*

When P.T.L. went down, there was much ridicule from the media and some of the families of those who contributed throughout the United States. I want this book to help these people feel good about their involvement, their decisions, and those of their friends. I want them to hold their heads high and be able to say, "Look at what has happened, what is still happening and what will happen in the future -- for God -- because of ministries of P.T.L!"

Ray and Margia Walters

Chapter 1

GOD'S GLOW

Ray and Margia's Story

*D*ear Reader,
 All of us watched the reports on television and read over and over again about the disturbing happenings at P.T.L. It was sensational news in the beginning. Everyone's eyes were glued to the newspapers and television screens waiting to hear the latest on Jim and Tammy Faye. Time has now caused the cameras to go on to more newsworthy scenes. They don't realize that there are still stories hidden within the ruins of former P.T.L. -- stories more compelling than any of the head liners that appeared at the downfall. The criticism from the media, the shame and embarrassment of being pointed out as part of Heritage Village, the ridicule of friends and relatives, and the self-doubts and questioning were enough to make many wonder. I have gradually become more and more aware of God's complete plan. I know now why he placed me in the middle of all that was going on during both the good times and the bad. It was so that I would be able to tell the "whole" story -- to complete the account of P.T.L.
 While my wife, Margia, and I were living in San Antonio, Texas, we watched the P.T.L. programs on television and were attracted to the good that was being done. Since we were suppliers to the Christian Booksellers Convention at the time, we decided to visit P.T.L. on our way to the convention in D.C. Our first visit to the grounds astounded us. The landscaping, the buildings, the facilities were

"Mr. Noah" (otherwise known as Ray Walters) and Sean Webb with the Mr. Noah puppet she made in her puppet ministry.

beautiful. Even more beautiful was the feeling of love and acceptance that permeated the entire place.

When it came time for us to leave for the convention, we couldn't get Heritage out of our minds. Neither Margia nor I said anything for the first several miles. Then suddenly we both spoke at the same time. "We have to go back!" It was like a rubber band was pulling us back to that wonderful atmosphere and the love and safety we had felt while we were there.

After we arrived home, we watched P.T.L. continuously. One day Tammy Faye was playing with some toys on stage when Margia and I decided the people at P.T.L. needed to see the Christian talking dolls we distributed. We called Charlotte Whiting, the Promotions and Projects Director at P.T.L., and made an appointment to show her our dolls. She, in turn, shared with us a rendering of the P.T.L. complex as it would be when completed. In one day, we signed a lease for a toy store on the grounds and a contract for a house to be built in the Mulberry Village Subdivision.

Our lifestyle changed dramatically. There were such genuine

expressions of friendship among the people. Everyone was welcome. This was a place where a person could really become closer to God in his or her daily living. Everyday problems were still there, of course, but they seemed somehow easier to handle. We knew God had called us there. There were delays in finishing both the house and the store, so we set up a temporary shop in trailers and the recreation building. In 1985, our store was finally ready. Noah's Toy Shoppe opened on Main Street of Heritage Village in February of 1985.

That morning, Jim and Tammy brought the television cameras into the store and aired our products all over the United States. I was carrying a duck puppet, demonstrating it for the cameras, and within three days, we had so many orders for toys that we had to hire an extra person just to take the telephone orders. In eleven months, we sold $740,000 worth of toys in 1400 square feet of space. Thousands of people visited P.T.L. and most of them came in our store.

Things went so well that we expanded our shops into Texas, Alabama, Florida and Tennessee. Margia and I took trips to Nuremberg, Germany; Tokyo, Japan; Seoul, Korea; and Switzerland to buy special toys. Our toys were nonviolent and many of them were named after Bible characters.

During this time, Margia and I were also doing volunteer work and becoming a part of the community. In 1986, I began to see problems arising. I knew in my spirit that God would not tolerate some of the things that were happening. When Jim resigned, tempers flared and people took sides. Many were hurt. Our business began to crumble along with P.T.L., but as president of the Main Street Merchants Association, I tried to keep things functioning with the new people. Fear took over many lives. People didn't know what was going to happen to them and their families. Criticisms grew. Bankruptcy and judges entered the picture.

Somehow in the midst of all the criticism, the good facets of P.T.L. were lost, buried beneath layers of shame and sneering. After the closing of our store, Margia and I moved back to San Antonio, Texas, to continue our life with our family. When I later moved back to South Carolina and received God's direction to write this book, He began to open doors. From that point on, I barely had to tap on a door, and it was flung wide open. There was no doubt that

Noah's Toy Shoppe

Inside Noah's Toy Shoppe

God had been there before me. Every single person I contacted was excited that God was allowing me to tell the real story.

I pray this book will be an answer to those who questioned. I pray it will help calm those who criticized and relieve those who were hurt. It is my dream that it will touch the hearts of thousands and encourage their faith in God. Through these pages, I want the world to see the good that has come out of P.T.L. and lasted long after the bad has died away.

These are the stories worthy of our attention. They are the tales of the care-givers and project planners, the soul-seekers, and out-reachers who lived and worked at P.T.L. and Heritage Village.

This book is for you, the innocents, who are scattered throughout the world now -- performing God's work quietly -- without the fanfare or cameras. May these pages be a hand of healing that reaches from one heart to another and brings forgiveness, reconciliation and peace.

We love you all,
Ray and Margia Walters

Chapter 2

GLORIOUS GEMS

God's Special Children

As proprietor of Noah's Toy Shoppe, I had the God-given privilege of meeting many of the people who came to visit P.T.L. Some of them came to the grounds simply to praise God. Others came to find solutions to problems that plagued them or their loved ones. Many had questions and were looking for answers.

Kevin's House

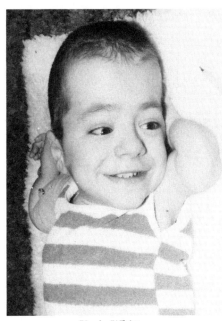
Kevin Whittum

Whatever their reasons, I was blessed by everyone, who came into our store. The greatest blessings, however, came from God's special children who came to visit. These individuals, from the youngest to the oldest, stole our hearts. Some were physically disabled, either by birth or through an accident, but they were also blessed and gifted by God in other extraordinary ways. We are all God's children as Christians, but these people were definitely God's "Special Children" in the way they were able to touch those with whom they came in contact.

It would take too many pages to tell of all the feelings and privileges that we had as owners of the toy store in dealing with these special individuals, but we would like to include letters from some of these individuals and/or their families.

Kevin Whittum was one such individual. Although he was physically disabled, Kevin had a brilliant mind. I remember Kevin suggesting several times that we should go into business together. He loved our Toy Shoppe. Of course when the downfall of P.T.L. came, that opportunity was no longer available. A large building was erected on the grounds in his honor to house disabled children. "Kevin's House" was built in record time for its size and nature and was dedicated to the housing of children like Kevin.

This first letter is from Kevin's family, David Whittum, Barb Peterson, Kathleen Anderson and their families:

Carolyn Whittum

Dear Reader,

The building of Kevin's House was a dream come true for our parents, Reverend David and Ione Whittum as well as for our brother Kevin and sister Carolyn. Kevin and Carolyn had been touching people and amazing doctors with their hearts full of love all their lives. Mom and Dad had been ministering to children all their married lives. Their home was filled with love. Kevin's House was a dream come true in that Mom and Dad would now have the ability to help many more children in this beautiful, huge home and share with others the specialness of forgotten children.

Kevin and Carolyn's national exposure spoke of hope and encouragement for many people around the country. Many parents, who had special children of their own, called, wrote letters to, and visited the Whittums. The responsibility can seem overwhelming and speaking to someone who's handling it successfully was really a blessing. I remember a call they received from a family who had an infant son with the same disease as Kevin. The doctors offered so little. Mom and Dad visited them. They began to see the blessings and potentials instead of just the problems.

Many children around the country have received that love and attention because Kevin's House and all the national attention drawn on Kevin and Carolyn encouraged and inspired others around the country to open homes of love for special children. Here in Grand Rapids, Michigan, David's House was opened. We still frequently see their van around town -- full of God's kids.

Kevin went to be with his Lord in August 1992. Ione (Mom) Whittum passed away November 1992; and Reverend Whittum (Dad) joined them in May 1997. We miss them greatly!

> The Whittum Family
> David Whittum, Barb Peterson,
> Kathleen Anderson & Families

Another special young man was Bryon Sparks who had a rare skin disease that prevented people from touching him. Bryon fought Epidermolysis Bullosa Dystrophica from the day he was born. This disease which causes the skin to blister and peel at the slightest touch, affects one in 600,000 children. Through hearing his story, I cried more than I had in years as my heart went out to him, his parents, grandparents, and family. As a vessel of God he was responsible for bringing many thousands of young people to the Lord.

Our next letter is from Lillian Sparks, the mother of Bryon Sparks. Much of this information is taken from tapes by his family and from the books *Tough Cookie* (ISBN 0-89221-198-9) and *Parents Cry Too* (ISBN 0-89221-182-2). They have given us permission to tell you their story. (If you would like to order either book, you may do so through Lillian Sparks at 2328 Linda Drive, NW, Warren OH 44485.)

Bryon's father, Stephen, tells us first about looking for his son when he was born through the hospital nursery window:

My eyes moved from one bassinet to another searching for my son. Then out of the corner of my eye, I saw the most pitiful scene of humanity. What was it? A burn case -- a rare condition of leprosy -- a baby perhaps boiled alive in a tub of scalding water -- or the product of child abuse? Isolated near the wall, the sterile incubator contained a screaming mass of purple flesh covered with large, blood-filled blisters over the hands, feet, knees, buttocks, scalp, and face. More than 80 percent of the body surface was either lesioned or denuded of skin. Several pieces of epidermis had peeled back and were hanging on by mere threads.

An unexplainable wave of compassion swept over my pastoral heart. Right there I bowed my head and prayed for God to heal the child and give his parents supernatural strength to face the situation. I brushed the tears from my cheeks as I raised my eyes to search for "my little boy." Ironically at that instant, a nurse walked over to the suffering infant, wheeled the isolette around, opened the portholes, and began to administer a medication. In a fraction of a second, a blue-card attached to the hidden side of the incubator burned these words into my brain, 'Baby Boy Sparks.'"

And now, we'll hear from Bryon's mother, Lillian.

Dear Reader,

Usually a child with this disease does not survive past the first 24 hours. If they do, they are handicapped severely, and Bryon made it longer than most. He was a blue-eyed, bright, bubbly, very determined young man. Through his uncountable sufferings and courageous spirit, he taught many people the meaning of simple faith.

He once told me, "I was just talking to Jesus about healing my body. It's okay, Mom. He is going to make me better."

Bryon was first given the nickname of "Bright Cookie," because of his sweet disposition, his clear, alert mind, and the way he was able to "eat his way" into people's hearts.

Tough Cookie — Bryon Todd Sparks (Photo by Steve Hulbert).

With the determination of a fighter written on his face, Bryon rounds a bend on his "Big Wheels." (Photo by Steve Hulbert.)

It was later changed to "Tough Cookie" by his doctor for obvious reasons. Bryon's complete outer skin and every internal organ and mucous membrane with the exception of his colon was affected with a rare and incurable disease. Twice every day, he had to be covered with a special Silvadene Cream and wrapped with yards of Vaseline gauze and bandages to protect the open and bloody sores that covered his body.

Doctors said he would never survive past six months or if he did, that he would be little more than a vegetable. They predicted that he would never be right mentally because of the large amount of drugs that he had to take, but all of us refused to accept these predictions. We knew that somehow God would intervene and change our lives.

Despite it all, Bryon grew up as a bright, happy, determined child with a cheerful disposition. On March 9, 1982, the producers from the P.T.L. Television Network arranged to fly Bryon, his father and me from our home in East Providence, Rhode Island, to Charlotte, North Carolina, to make the first of what would be many national television appearances. By that time, both Steve and I were on the teaching faculty of Zion Bible Institute, a "faith" school that did not charge its students for room, board, or tuition.

Our family was not receiving a regular source of income, so we had to trust God to supply our needs. While in Charlotte, we stayed in the P.T.L. Mansion and were asked to appear on the television program with the Bakkers talking about Bryon's traumatic beginning and consequent struggles.

We told the P.T.L. audience about a time shortly after Bryon learned to walk when he was strolling along with his dad and tripped. Steve grabbed his coat sleeve and accidentally grasped the skin on Bryon's arm. Like a playtex glove, the entire outer layer of skin came off from the elbow down. Miraculously, however, within ten days, with treatment and God's healing, new skin covered his entire arm and hand. We told of Bryon's difficulty in swallowing by the time he was three and of his steadily losing weight and energy. We told of surgeries to replace his damaged esopha-

gus and of several more "degloving" accidents which caused Bryon's fingers to grow together into fused mittens of skin.

We also told them that Bryon had learned to write despite this handicap and to ride a two-wheel bike, shoot basketball, and play soccer, do his schoolwork and help around the house. By that time, Jim's polished professionalism had broken down. His eyes were moist and he struggled to contain himself. Tammy Faye and Uncle Henry were openly weeping. Jim attempted to collect his thoughts and asked, "What are Bryon's plans for the future? Does he have any dreams?"

"Yes, God has given Bryon a wonderful dream for the future," I replied. "You can see that Bryon's hands and fingers are contracted into useless mittens of skin. Even though three separate operations have been performed, none of them have been successful. About a year ago Bryon came into our room and told us that the Lord had given him a dream - his pajamas had fallen off and new skin covered his body -- but best of all -- he had ten brand new fingers to raise to the Lord!"

As the cameras zoomed in, with a close up of Bryon's bandaged hand and scarred, useless right hand, the studio audience exploded with applause and cheers. They were saying, "Bryon, you're a brave boy and we believe in you. One day God will bring your dream to pass."

When Bryon was asked to sing a song, the P.T.L. audience and the Bakkers fell even more in love with him. Later, Steve and I sent the P.T.L. Network and the Bakkers a thank you note and mentioned that we had learned of a hospital in Germany which could possibly help Bryon. It wasn't long until the producers called to tell us that Jim was going to read the letter over the air and that they were sending us a check for $40,000 to pay for Bryon's treatment.

A few months prior to that time, Bryon had written the following letter and left it on our pillows:

Dear Dad,

Thank you so much for talking to me earlier today. I learned a lot about what you said of death. Death will be my very best friend. I just want to be healed so bad, Dad. I've asked God so many times 2 very important questions.

1. When will I be healed?

2. If God doesn't heal me, when will I die and go to heaven to meet my healer?

Lately, I've just felt so lonely for heaven, Dad. I'm just so tired of fighting! I've accomplished a lot down here ... you're right. But like you said, Dad, "To live is Christ, but to die is gain."

When I die, I want to die in my sleep ... to see the light at the end of a dark long tunnel ... and then to see heaven, my home sweet home with Jesus.

I promise to get things ready in heaven for you and my family, if I die first. Which I'm ready to go Dad. I AM READY!

My trust is in God. May his will be done in my life ... so it will be the easiest for me. Whatever happens in the future... just remember ... I love you Dad and Mom!

Your son, Bryon

<u>*P.S. You can share this with Mom.*</u>

Through the rest of his life, Bryon helped to keep our entire family's priorities in focus. Often he would say to us, "Every day is a gift from God. I'm so glad to be alive! ... Mom I want you to know that I appreciate you and Dad. I realize that I am alive today because you guys have hung in there for me. When everyone else gave up on me and said I couldn't make it ... you and Dad believed in God ... I know it was your faith that has kept me alive ... and I want to thank you."

Lillian Sparks

The next letter is from Bryon's sister, Jenell Sparks:

Dear Reader,
Everything about my life has been rather ordinary. I am an average high school freshman with mediocre grades and the customary friends. I live in an average town amid a mediocre neighborhood with the customary family. Well, customary, that is except for my brother, Bryon.

Nothing about his life has been ordinary. At birth the doctors discovered he had an incurable disease which we call E.B. for short. The doctors didn't give him twenty-four hours, but through God's miraculous touch, he lived 21½ years. It was on this past November 5, 1995, at 6:30 a.m. that his spirit left his body. It happened to be on a Sunday. Of course, it would be. That was Bryon's favorite day of the week. He savored the opportunity he had as a Sunday School teacher of 9, 10, and 11-year-olds, to teach them God's Word. After all, he was a living example of it.

Bryon also loved the worship service. It seems that his whole life was a praise to the Lord. That's what made Bryon so extraordinary, his spirit. But let me back up a few months to relate the events that would transform my ordinary life into a not-so-ordinary one, when I caught Bryon's spirit.

Last January an unusual growth appeared on his hand. My parents worried about it, but they didn't do anything right away, hoping it would gradually go away. But it didn't. In fact, doctors injected a needle into Bryon's lung to remove some liquid surrounding the cavity. It was sent to lung specialists.

I will never forget how I was told the news. My sister, LeeAnn, and I had just gotten off our bus from school on a Wednesday in October. As soon as we walked into the house, I saw my dad and younger brother, Brent sitting in the living room waiting for us. We sat down. Dad told us the news that was going to change our lives forever. He reached for his heart, and in tears said, "Bryon has cancer. It has spread throughout one lung and could be anywhere else!" I felt like somebody had just slapped me. All I remember is that I began to cry. I was unaware that those tears would become very familiar to me in the next few months.

Bryon was unable to have lung surgery and could not withstand chemotherapy because of his skin disease. It was Bryon's desire to come home and eventually the doctors released him, because there was nothing more they could do. He was able to swing in the backyard one more time, lay beside "Higgins," his dog, and give us our Christmas gifts.

He was given morphine to reduce the pain, and another strong medicine to control the nausea. Even though the medication caused him to drift in and out of consciousness, it seemed that during Bryon's last days he appeared the keenest, especially in his knowledge of God. Just sitting there listening to what he had to say made me feel like I was listening to God himself.

I remember vividly one particular time when my family was talking to Bryon during his last days. He looked straight at me and said, "Jenell, I'm scared that you might not go to Heaven." That's when it clicked. How stupid I had been! So caught up in my own world, I didn't even stop to listen to anybody. It took someone on his death bed for me to come around. I'm ashamed of that, but I'm also grateful he said it. If he hadn't cared about my spiritual life, I don't know where I would be right now. I totally turned back to God. I had tried to live a lukewarm life, but that's not good enough for God.

This is the story of my very ordinary, yet not-so-ordinary, life. The last few days of Bryon's life had to have been the hardest, for my family and for him. We thought he would die so many times, but his heart kept beating strong. It was totally unbelievable that he lived as long as he did. But that last day ... it will stick out in my mind forever. I was with Bryon almost the whole day, Saturday, November 4th. At one point that day, I went and lay next to him on his bed. He was hardly breathing. He was deep in a coma, so I wasn't really sure if he even realized that I was there. I ran my hand through his hair and put my other hand next to his amputated arm. That's when he lifted *his shortened arm and put it in my hand to let me know that he realized I was there. I sat and held him, trying to convince him that it would be all right. A person feels so helpless when they're staring death in the face. I kissed him numerous times, thinking that he looked like a victim of the holocaust; he was skin and bones. Just a few hours later, he died, peacefully, without a struggle. For this, I thank the Lord.*

Every day we must face the sorrow and the grief, and remind ourselves that he is definitely in a better place. Even though we miss him, we'll always have the wonderful memory of this brave young man. Bryon was such a warrior, such a soldier, such a "Tough Cookie." His spirit was strong, even until the end. Thank you Bryon, for letting me catch your spirit.

Love From Bryon's Sister,
Jenell Sparks

The following letter is made up of excerpts from an interview with Pastor and Mrs. Richardson, the grandparents of Bryon:

Dear Reader,

Bryon was our first grandchild, so it was very hard for us to understand why this terrible thing had happened to him. When he was about eight years old, he and his family were invited to come to P.T.L. He sang "I'll give my hands to you, my heart to you," on the program. After that, they sent them to Germany where a biochemist was able to give him special treatments, vitamins, and diets that almost completely eradicated the sores for many years. If it hadn't been for that, I don't believe Bryon would have lived beyond those eight years.

P.T.L. later sent him to Spain and Italy for more treatments and operations. Because they were willing to give more than $80,000 toward the cost of treatments for my grandson, he was able to live until a year ago November. We thank the Lord that he was able to become a great witness for God and win many, many people to Christ before *he died. Young people were saved, doctors, even an airline pilot who piloted one of the planes on which they traveled. Once as a young teen, he spoke at the Brooklyn Tabernacle and more than 400 young people gave their hearts to Jesus Christ in that service.*

God used Bryon's life to touch people. He could sing perfect pitch, and by the time he was three, he had memorized thirty choruses. In the hospital, they'd carry him around in a little red cart, and he'd sing "God is so Good." Of course, it took a lot of love and care for Bryon. The other three children were normal even though the doctors said they wouldn't be; and Bryon went to school even though the doctors said he could never learn. He always got A's and wrote with beautiful penmanship. He graduated with honors from high school and was going to college by correspondence. Just before he passed away, the state of Pennsylvania sent him a certificate saying they were awarding him a teacher's certificate because he was such a good teacher.

*Bryon's Grandfather,
Pastor Richardson*

Another special individual was Brent Rahlf, who always came into our store with a smile and great anticipation. He loved us and we loved him. The next is a letter from the Rahlf family in which they tell us a little of what it was like to be the parents of one of God's "Special Children" at P.T.L.

Dear Reader,

Greetings in Jesus' name! Do you mind if we share a little nostalgia? As I write, we are traveling to California from our home in Oregon and listening to a cassette tape by Derek Floyd, who was, years ago, one of the P.T.L. singers at Heritage U.S.A. It brings back fond memories of our visits there. We lived in Wisconsin during that time. We can still feel the synergy of that wonderful place as we listen.

Heritage U.S.A. was a place we could take our physically and mentally challenged little five-year-old son, Brent,

Brent Rahlf on the grounds

and our grown children. We always felt welcome and enjoyed our times there. The sights and sounds were uplifting to us all. From the drive up, where we were greeted by Norm the doorman, to the last goodbye three nights and four days later, we were treated like royalty by servants of the King!

Our purpose for visits to Heritage was to support a much needed Christian resort and to enjoy a first class vacation complete with family members and the fellowship of other Christians. It fulfilled all of those desires and more.

One morning as we were observing the production of the daily TV program at the Studio, we met a kind lady usher whose name was Michael. She took us to a not-so-conspicuous seat in the event Brent would need a break, and when he did, Michael aptly helped him down the tiered stairway. We established an acquaintance which has endeared her to us for sixteen years. This lasting friendship has meant so much to our entire family. We have prayed through times of need and shared many joys. Though many miles separate us, we are always near in spirit and via wireless! Michael introduced us to many fine folk at the restaurants and shops on Main Street U.S.A.

Ray Walters and his wife Margie, proprietors of the Toy Shoppe, were two of those special people. Brent couldn't wait to get to the Toy Shoppe. Ray always greeted him with some wonderful creation pulled out of his sleeve or from behind him. One of his favorites was a top-of-the-line impeccably dressed Mickey Mouse. Brent still has it, of course. Ray and Margie were and still are truly God's servants.

Before we came to Heritage, we had heard about another young man whose name was Kevin. I'm sure many of you knew him, too. Brent felt empathy for Kevin and wanted to meet him, because he too had great physical challenges. One day Michael took us to Kevin's House, a specially equipped home built to accommodate a number of special needs' children and Brent visited with Kevin. This became a highlight of all of our times at Heritage.

Michael Miller, Brent, "Mom", and Brent's Older Sister, Charlane

Brent & Doorman

Horse & Carriage With Brent

Brent, Mom & Dad at the Studio

The Petting Zoo was a fun place near Kevin's House. Brent loved to ride with family members in the horse drawn carriage. After long and very full days of train rides, miniature golf, swimming and fellowship with new friends, we often stopped to get a late-night snack at the lower level of the Grand Hotel. There was always some type of informal entertainment. Guitar "pickin' and singing," keyboard, or some light comedy. It was a relaxing place to stop after the evening service at The Barn.

We were so fond of the ministry of Bob and Jeanne, Mike Murdock, David Ingles, The Goodmans, Doug Oldham, Lulu Roman and all of the P.T.L. singers. They added much to the services. Now we can watch them on the videos and feel like we've known them for all these years.

We had never been to see a passion play anywhere before, so it was good to be able to attend the "best" Passion Play first. It was rated number one in all the land, and was so moving. On the practical side, Brent's dad re-

minds us of how big and comfortable the beds were at the hotel. How could you possibly enjoy all those amenities without a good night's sleep?

It has been good to be able to share our experiences at Heritage with you. We were sorry that the Resort had to close, but neither our faith nor our trust in God or His people was daunted. It was a little bit of what Heaven perhaps will be like ... beautiful people, wholesome activity, and a oneness of spirit to Praise the Lord. We always left feeling that we had received more than we had given.

The Rahlf Family

The following letter is from Thelma Pointkowski in Ft. Mill, South Carolina and tells of their Downs Syndrome daughter, "Sharon," another of God's Special Children. She is called an angel and has a sweet smile at all times. Today, Sharon is a healthy 34-year-old "delight," despite what her mother calls "a real stubbornness." Thelma lives near the old entrance and is involved in Prison Ministry, counseling and trying to help those who have come out of prison to have a new life. Everyone was so loving and accepting of Thelma and her daughter Sharon at P.T.L. Perhaps that's part of the reason Thelma is so eager to love and accept other people today who are handicapped in a different way.

Dear Reader,

My husband, Joe, and I moved to Wilmington in 1977 from New Jersey near Philadelphia, Pennsylvania. Then I came to Heritage U.S.A. from Wilmington, North Carolina, in July of 1987.

Our daughter, Sharon, has Down Syndrome, a birth defect which causes retardation. At birth Sharon had a severe blockage in the large intestine which caused severe vomiting. As she grew older, she ate very little because the food would build up and not pass into the stomach.

When she was fourteen months old, she only weighed six pounds. Sharon probably would have died except for her strong heart and the fact that God had other plans for her. I was told she was a "poor specimen" and psychotic.

Thelma & Sharon Pointkowski

Out of fear and frustration, I called my sister and told her I was watching Sharon die. She was in an infant seat, had no energy, couldn't hold her head up or do anything, and hardly ever even cried. She slept next to our bed where I kept a vigil all night.

My sister gave me the name of a caring doctor. When I took Sharon to him and watched him pick her up and hug her to him, I cried. I cried again later when I had to leave her at the hospital for tests. That was when they discovered her blockage, and my husband and I decided to take her to Children's Hospital in Philadelphia. Our pastor came with us to the hospital and tried to convince us that we had to give her up to the Lord. I couldn't do it at first, but once I realized that she belonged to the Lord, I was finally able to release her to Him. Shortly thereafter, our doctor came out and said she was doing well and had a peachy color. From then on we saw physical progress.

The year, Sharon was fifteen, my husband died of Melanoma Cancer. It was a hard time for me. Another daughter and her husband lived in the Meadows and loved P.T.L. They felt so secure living on the grounds with their two children, Mary and Joseph. I decided to buy a home in Dogwood Manor for myself and Sharon so we could be with family.

My grandson was dedicated at the old P.T.L. church, and I had such wonderful experiences of seeing my family's delight as we walked the grounds, rode the train, visited the Goody Barn and Noah's Toy Shoppe on Main Street. We ate our favorite ice cream in the old fashioned ice cream parlor, and it was a wonderful life.

Thelma Pointkowski

Brooke Roberts was a special little girl from Houston Texas. She was brought into the store by her Grandmother Rene Roberts. Brooke became close friends with Bob and Jeannie Johnston, and the families still visit every year. This letter is from Rene Roberts and tells about Brooke, who became "Little Miss Heritage U.S.A." and sang with the P.T.L. singers. Their family started going to P.T.L. in 1985 when Brooke was five years old. They stayed in the Grand Hotel, the "cabins" and at the campground for several weeks at a time. The grandchildren enjoyed the train, old cars, paddle boats, fishing and especially the carousel.

The first time Brooke rode the carousel, they had a hard time getting her off. After about twelve times around, she fell asleep, and they decided she'd had enough. Today Brooke is sixteen years old.

Dear Reader,

We became acquainted with Bob and Jeanne Johnson during our first trip to P.T.L. They fell in love with Brooke, and on our visits afterwards, they would have her on their television broadcasts, the camp meetings, and the dinner theater. This relationship turned into a lasting friendship. We're still in touch, and they have spent a week at a time in our home here in South Houston.

They took Brooke under their wings. She learned their songs and had them as wonderful role models for

Brooke Roberts — 6 Years Old

Bob and Jeanne Johnson With Brooke and Derek Floyd at Dinner Theater

Brooke Singing Butterfly Song

Brian Keith, P.T.L. Singer & Brooke

Art, Brooke and Gene on a Float "Little Miss Heritage U.S.A."

Brooke Singing With P.T.L. Singers

her singing. P.T.L. opened many doors for Brooke to watch great performers and hear a lot of good teaching. She loved the Passion Play. We all thought it was a great performance. But her delight was to visit the P.T.L. singers. Her "boyfriend" at that time was Brian Keith.

So many were interested in praying for Brooke, because of her C.P., and she loved going to the Upper Room. She sang "No Ground" with Derek Floyd, a great guy! And other friends of hers were Doug Oldham, the door men, the shopkeepers, and hotel staff. Everyone there seemed to be of one mind and all loved the Lord and wanted to be in a place where others had the same interests.

At Christmas time, it was a winter wonderland. Brooke enjoyed spending time with little Kevin and Carolyn. They had lots of laughs and good times together. What an opportunity for a little girl like Brooke to have shared and been a part of such a wonderful place and people. She will always have beautiful memories. Those were our "highlight" years.

Rene Roberts

Dear Mr. Wolters,

   I am so sorry that it has taken me a long time to write you and tell you about my time in PTL so you can add it to your book. Here is my opinion of PTL.

   My first time to go to PTL was in the summer of 1986. I can still remember the first time I stood in front of the "Heritage USA" sign to have my picture taken by my grandmother.

   I made so many friends at PTL and to tell you the truth, they were just like family. When I met Bob and Jeanne Johnson, I remember how they just took me under their wings and how we became such close "buddies". Singing "We Have This Moment" with them on television for the first time at the age of 5, I can remember was a great experience as well as many other times. I had so many friends at PTL that I could never name. All of them, but some of my closest friends, just to name a few were "The P.T.L. Singers", but I must add that Brian Keith was my "boyfriend" the years I went to PTL. Kevin and Carol were some other close friends as well as Charlie. Art the doorman and all the people on "Main Street" were also very friendly. Sometimes people would come up to me and talk, but I never would know their name.

    Some of my favorite things to do were ride the tram and train as well as the "merry-go-round." One of my favorite things to do around Christmas time was to go look at all the Christmas lights!

    Some of my favorite places to go were the "candy store" in which I would always get a sample of vanilla candy every day.

Another place I went to a lot was the ice cream store in which I would always order black cherry ice cream on a sugar cone. The toy store was also a fascinating place. The waterpark was something I always looked forward to because of the cool water, fun slides, and friendly people. I loved to go and see the passion play and sometimes I wondered if the man acting out the part of Jesus, ever got hurt during the "crucifiction" (did I spell it right?)

One of my most favorite things to go to was the dinner theater. Some of my favorite shows include "Bob & Jeanne Always", "Sing, America, Sing", "Love Came Down" and "The Greatest Gift Of All". I loved the food and the shows were always fantastic!

I remember all the studio broadcasts that would take place and all the times I sang including the time when the P.O.O.K. family came to P.T.L. in their animal costumes. I remember singing "Anchors Away" while the P.O.O.K. family danced in the background.

I remember being baptized in the Hotel lobby pool which was a great experience. Riding in the hotel elevators with the glass window was something I also enjoyed. As the years passed, I made so many memories of P.T.L. which will never be forgotten and the times that I spent there will always be cherished.

It has been eleven years now since I came to P.T.L. for the first time and it seems just as if it was yesterday. I am 16 years old now and I am a junior at Deer Park High School in Deer Park, TX. Even though I'm older now I'll never forget my favorite place called P.T.L.

Love always, Brooke Roberts

Chapter 3

PRECIOUS PRAYER

The Upper Room

The Upper Room was (and is) a prayer chapel and one of the most important and largest mines on the grounds of Heritage U.S.A. Diamonds and treasures were plentifully supplied by God twenty-four hours a day. There is certainly power through agreement in prayer, and there was always someone in the Upper Room to share that power.

Heritage U.S.A.'s Upper Room opened in 1982. Many people would come to P.T.L. to attend the workshops, seminars, and camp meetings, and eventually end up at the Upper Room to pray and be prayed for by the full time pastors. The Upper Room is still available for prayer today.

The building is fashioned after the original Upper Room found in Jerusalem with a stone surfaced exterior and an interior set with large white columns. There are wooden benches for seating and windows of colored glass. There are also prayer closets where those in need can commune with God privately.

Louis Campbell was one of the pastors in the Upper Room who saw many won for Christ. He remembers witnessing numerous healings and seeing people brought back from the brink of suicide. Neither he, the other pastors, nor the thousands of visitors will ever forget their experiences in the Upper Room. They are still counting their blessings.

The Upper Room

The following letter is taken from an interview with Pastor Richardson who ministered at the Upper Room:

Dear Reader,

I came to P.T.L. because I felt a great compassion for reaching, hurting people. When I saw that P.T.L. was a place where thousands of hurting people were coming, needing love and compassion, I decided to come as the Senior Pastor at the Upper Room.

The Upper Room was a very special ministry. It was common for us to have seven to eight communion and healing services every day. Many miracles happened. One woman came with cancer in her ear and was miraculously healed. Another sister, Sandra Gardner, had M.S. and came to the Upper Room for healing. The doctors had given up hope of ever helping her. The first night we prayed with her, she was healed of a rare eye disease. The next night while she was watching others being prayed for, she began walking the Walk of Faith with her nurse, Diana. Suddenly she was running around the Walk of Faith, shouting, "I'm healed, I'm healed!" When she returned to her home and church, people realized she'd had a miracle to happen in her life.

The Walk of Faith was a very important part of the Upper Room. As people walked the Walk of Faith, they could read the beautiful scriptures of healing and victory which were inscribed in the walkway. By the time they reached the Upper Room, many of them had faith to believe for miracles in their lives.

Another woman came with cancer of the eyelid. We prayed and on the way home, when she stopped in a little hotel room and washed her face, the growth fell in the sink. The doctor who examined her later verified that she had been healed. One man, Bob Harris, who had a large hernia in the groin area, stood asking for prayer in the large crowd. Later he came back to tell us that two days later, the hernia began going down and by the time he got back to Ohio, the hernia and his rheumatoid arthritis was gone.

Prayer Bin in Upper Room Full of Prayer Requests

Statue in Front of Upper Room

During the five years I was there, an average of 100,000 people passed through the Upper Room each year. Busloads came from Pennsylvania, Ohio, and Michigan for the workshops and seminars, the Passion Play, and the wonderful prayer ministry of the Upper Room.

I would never trade those years that I ministered to people in the Upper Room. It was common to see people come there to the prayer closets and pray all night. Some stayed for two weeks praying and seeking God. At one time, during a four month period, I had 37 pastors and evangelists who came to the Upper Room, ready to give up the ministry. They would stay in the little cubicles, crying and praying. I had gone through great sorrow in my own pastoral ministry at one time, so I could relate to them and was able to help bring healing, comfort and direction to them. I had an opportunity to counsel them, and 85% of them decided to go back into the ministry. They found new hope and courage, not because of me, but because they came to the Upper Room to seek God.

When Hurricane Hugo came, the grounds were torn up, but I managed to keep the Upper Room open with candlelight for a week. There was no electricity, but people climbed over the damage to come in for prayer. I cut the trees away with a chain saw so they could get in. There was so much damage that we had to close after a week. I stayed on and helped with the telephone services.

We had a prayer bin which held an average of 500,000 prayer requests, and we would pray over those prayer requests every day. We received hundreds and hundreds of letters where prayers were answered, and we had thousands of pictures of loved ones that people had placed there so others would be reminded to pray for them.

People kept coming, even through all the problems. They came in broken, some were employees fired on the job because the place was going down, desperate, crying. We'd pray for them and peace and new hope would come. The Upper Room remained a place of healing and a place where one could feel God's presence as long as the doors were open. There's no way to count the numbers of people who were helped by the ministries they received there -- and no way to count the numbers of people who went out from there to minister to others.

Pastor Richardson

The Walk of Faith at the Upper Room

The following letter was written by Robert Gafflin from Wenonah, New Jersey. Mr. and Mrs. Gafflin are members of Time-Share at Lakeside Lodges and have been married for 41 years. Mrs. Gafflin is suffering from dementia, so on their latest visit to the grounds, during the week of June 21 - 28, 1997, they once again walked the Walk of Faith, trusting and believing God for another miracle in their lives. Robert laid hands upon his wife in the Upper Room and prayed a prayer of faith over her.

Dear Reader,

We first came to Heritage U.S.A. in 1980. Shortly afterwards on the verge of separating, we decided to give our marriage one more try ... at Heritage. And so it was, through taking the Walk of Faith, that the Lord met our needs and gave us what we needed to be able to reunite in Christ and make our marriage work.

Another time in 1985, I had been ill with pneumonia in the spring and couldn't quite shake it off. I had gone to the doctor and had x-rays and was to go back in a few days for another examination, but on the spur of the moment we decided to go down to Heritage for a few days to get away from it all. While there, we went to the Upper Room to attend one of the services. The speaker was from England, and he laid hands on me and prayed for my healing.

When we got back home, my daughter informed me that the doctor had called and asked me to come in immediately. When I arrived at his office, he said that the x-rays had shown fluid in my lung, and that it would have to be drained. I asked for another x-ray, and that one revealed that my lungs were clear with no trace of fluid. God had already healed me by the time the doctor called.

Robert Gafflin, Jr.

The next letter is from Pastor Dearborn:

Dear Reader,
  The first time I came, P.T.L. was located on Park Road in Charlotte. I came to visit my daughter and son-in-law who were working there. Lou Hostetler showed my wife and I the prayer phones and told us there were sixty and every one would be ringing back to back for two hours when the program started. He wanted my wife and me to help man the phones.
  That morning Corrie Ten Boom was on the program and calls came in from all over the country. During those two hours I was privileged to pray with people with all kinds of needs. Seventeen people gave their hearts to Jesus Christ. I told Nancy Negahaught, a young lady I'd had the privilege of baptizing when she was five years old, "I haven't had that many people saved in my church in the last three years."
  "Maybe God is calling you there," she told me.
  It wasn't long after that until I filled out an application. When Jeff Park called and offered me a job as a pastor/writer, we couldn't go because there wasn't a job for my wife. But in 1980, it was arranged for us to go with the School of Evangelism, taking twelve students to Jamaica for a month. We had services and Vacation Bible School. As time went on and Heritage U.S.A. began to develop, talk began about the Upper Room. Architects were sent to Jerusalem to measure that Upper Room in detail. The phone counseling was located in the lower part of the Upper Room after it was finished, and I was one of the counselors under the direction of Auber Sayer. I was later chosen to be the Day Pastor for the Upper Room.
  We had four or five paid pastors who worked eight hour shifts around the clock. These pastors would have communion three or four times a day. One afternoon, when I was the pastor on duty, we served communion to 1400 people from all over the country. As soon as one communion was finished, another would begin. One day a lady came in, brokenhearted over the death of her husband. She

couldn't get over the sorrow and grief. I prayed with her, we had communion, and after the service it was like a light came over her face. The lady with her said she hadn't seen a smile on her face for two years.

I was later assigned to another department in counseling and eventually I became the Pastor of Pastoral Care at Heritage Church. My wife worked in Pastoral Follow up. This was a tremendous ministry that contacted pastors from all over the nation when a call came in where someone needed a policeman, medical help or just someone to listen.

Today my prayer is that someone will turn these grounds once again into a place of ministry to hurting, needy people.

Your Friend in Christ
Pastor Bob Dearborn

The following letter is from Ernestine Bedford who worked on the phones in the Upper Room:

Mr. Ray

I've enjoy P.T.L. in the early 80. When I was in the Upper Room, working on the Phone, I would tell people, befor I let them go off the phone, that Jesus Love them, and the same sound Happen, and the same thing when I was ask on T.V. Phone. It was a Blessing to hear music all over the ground. Ernestine (Lena) Bedford

The next letter is from Col. Logan Weston who was one of the mainstays on the phone lines in the Upper Room. He says his experiences in life directly enabled him to assist the individual calls that came to his phones. He knows that God placed each call that he received especially to him. Col. Weston states, "God, in His providence, looks out for His own." This is shown clearly in the following passage from his book, *"The Fightin' Preacher"*:

Col. Logan Weston and Ray Walters

In searching the jungles after the skirmish, we found a wounded enemy soldier who had been shot out of a tree. He had been hit in the abdomen and was now lying unconscious on the ground. Our aid man, Joe Gomez, administered first aid, and when the prisoner regained consciousness, my Nisei Japanese interpreter, Sergeant Hank Gosho, began to interrogate him. We were interested in obtaining any information we could about the size, disposition, and armament of local units.

During the interrogation, the prisoner looked up and saw the chaplain's cross on my Bible, which I carried in a

> *cut-out canvas pouch on my ammunition belt. Startled, the prisoner asked the interpreter to ask me if I were a Christian. Yes. He then told the story of how three days earlier, he had set up his sniper post in a tree several miles further north. He saw the patrol coming down the trail, and as is common with snipers, he let the enlisted men pass with the hopes of taking out an officer. This would eliminate the leadership of the unit and, the Japanese hoped, bring chaos to the troops.*
>
> *As a sharpshooter, he had a four-power scope on his rifle, and he was rewarded for his patience when an officer came into his sights. He then asked the interpreter to ask me if I was there, and if I was the third man in that line. Yes, I was the third man in that column.*
>
> *He said he had pulled me into very short range, got a good sight picture on my head, and began to squeeze the trigger. Just then, the sun burst through a rift in the thick jungle canopy overhead. It hit the silver chaplain's cross on my Bible, and the cross zoomed out like a neon light, temporarily blinding him. When he saw that big bright cross there in the jungle and realized what had happened, he could not shoot. He assumed I was a Christian, and he himself had been converted at a mission station in Japan just before being drafted into the army.*

Further along in the same book, he tells of a similar experience:

> *One native guide (Beedy) and I crossed another large swamp and continued along the west bank of a small creek which drained into the swamp . . . I glanced to the right and there was a soldier just bringing his rifle into firing position . . . additional enemy troops in the area opened fire . . . We later returned to the other side of the swamp, where we washed off the mud and took inventory. One bullet had pierced my helmet just over my right eye. The bullet had sped around inside my helmet until it lost velocity. Another bullet had hit my shoe and lodged in the rubber heel. One had cut the watch right off my left wrist*

and left a burned place through my brand new jungle suit. That really made me mad. A burst of machine gun fire had torn the right pocket off my trousers, hit the grenade I carried there and glanced off, taking the rest of the grenades with it. And my Bible in my left breast pocket still held a bullet stopped right in the middle of the Psalms.

Col. Weston is now in the process of writing a new edition of his best-selling book, "*The Fightin' Preacher.*" You can contact him at his home (298 Swamp Fox Drive, Fort Mill, South Carolina 29715) for more information on how to receive the book. His personal letter to you, the Reader, follows:

Dear Reader,

Having completed a lengthy Army career and thirteen years tour of duty in the position of Coordinator of Religious Life at Texas A & M University, my wife and I decided to spend a two-week vacation at Heritage U.S.A. in South Carolina.

We drove our motor home to Ft. Mill and parked in the Sugar Creek Camping area. We enjoyed the television programs being conducted in the studio section of the Big Barn and the weekend services being conducted in the Big Barn Auditorium. It was here that we learned about the Upper Room and the Telephone counseling services being offered over the air waves. We volunteered to help answer phone calls asking for help in prayer coming from hungry hearts all over the world and specifically from the Americas, the Orient and Europe. This appeared to be a good place to spend our retirement years and to be of service to our fellow man. We were deeply impressed by the orderly fashion in which things were being conducted and also by the friendly, helpful attitude of the people.

Within the next year we sold our Texas property, bought a large, mobile home and relocated at Heritage. We immediately went to work on the phones often serving voluntarily for sixteen to eighteen hours a day. There was a bank of twenty-four phones, and they were ringing off the hook. One of the first calls that I responded to was from a crank who asked how much I was being paid. It was a pleasure to respond with "Not a red cent. I am just laying up treasures in Heaven." That was the last I ever heard from him.

Another call that came in that day was from a potential suicide. As a result of our phone conversation, she accepted Jesus as her Savior and departed rejoicing. Calls for healing and thanksgiving, as well as testimonies, flooded in. Surely God was doing great things. We were blessed.

Over the next two years, hundreds and hundreds of ailing hearts were helped, strengthened, encouraged, and motivated. This was a ministry truly blessed of the Lord. By 1989, Heritage began to crumble. The television programs began to fade out as did the Upper Room Prayer Chambers. Phone calls and prayer lines decreased until it was no longer considered feasible to keep the full time program operational. With dwindling help available, only part-time answering services were used. Eventually that too became minimal.

At about the time the phone service was phasing out, a program sponsored by Uncle Henry and Aunt Susan was gaining momentum. We were honored to be able to help with this testimonial style sharing program as long as Uncle Henry was able to continue.

Col. Logan Weston

The following letter is composed from an interview with Harry and Fran Fenwick, a dedicated couple who left their home in Pennsylvania recently to move to Fort Mill on "direct orders from God." Harry and Fran are two very precious people. Their only wish is to bring honor and glory to God.

Dear Reader,

The Lord has blessed us in so many ways. He allows us to show up. He does it all. We take no credit. It is a long story how we ended up here. We finally learned that if we will get quiet before the Lord, He will lead us directly. It all started in very non-significant ways that had nothing to do with where we are today other than possibly being obedient. He very clearly told us to come here and minister in the Upper Room, to be part of His ministry. He said that He would make the Upper Room available and He has done that.

When He told us to go to Fort Mill, S.C., we were not in the ministry. I was in sales, and all I knew was that I was feeling a "tug" and a love in my heart. One day I asked God to tell me what He wanted me to know. That's when He began to tell me, and I began to write it down. Today I have literally thousands of pages of instructions and guidance. It is amazing as I go back and read those pages to see what has happened. Through this experience, we have learned not to question Him anymore.

We don't just get out of bed in the morning now. We "roll out of bed on our knees" and surrender unto Jesus. He has absolutely done everything He has told us He would do. He said if you'll go and minister full time, I'll provide. We did, and He does. We have had to take some bold steps, but at no time have we ever felt like we had egg on our face or being made a fool of -- God won't do that. If the Lord is leading you, there's no pain. He had us contact some people and take some steps at times, which we would never have done on our own.

He has called us into a four-prong ministry, given us a mission statement which states we must work and witness so that lives may be saved. We also need to share and teach and provide a way whereby people of his choosing can learn the sweet communication there is inside. He has given us a healing ministry and blessed us with many results, and we feel He is asking us to provide a safe haven for His people. We are not sure exactly what that means yet, but we will know one of these days.

The most important thing that we see happening today is through the people who come through the door of the Upper Room. They are primarily nice, good Christian people. The Body of Christ is so torn up and hurt, however, that there's a terror and a darkness to these people when they come though the door. But as people pray and we share, you can almost see the joy and peace that come upon them. There's a shine to them when they walk out the door.

We have many pastors come in who contact us afterwards and tell us they feel a certain trust and a release of everything to Jesus. I can almost see a veil lift from people as joy comes upon them.

We left our home and family, but there have been no sacrifices. We have found, when we or anyone else chooses to follow Jesus 100%, the devil will attack. But just remember, Jesus always wins. I'm not sure what is going to happen with the Upper Room now. We are trying to put it all in His hands and just get out of the way. God sent us here, and He will give the increase. It has been awesome to see recognition come of the power of the Lord.

Harry and Fran Fenwick

Chapter **4**

RADIATING RICHES

Prison Ministry

C. O. P. E. (COALITION OF PRISON EVANGELISTS)

In my search for Hidden Treasures at P.T.L., I met and talked with Jeff Park who is the National Executive Director of C.O.P.E, another outreach mission of P.T.L. Jeff and I had lived next door to each other in Mulberry Village at P.T.L. He was a quiet individual, not pretentious, but totally dedicated to serving the Lord in Prison Ministry.

During my research for the book, Jeff asked if I would like to go to Columbia, S.C., to the State Prison on Easter Sunday for a sunrise service. When we arrived at the prison, security was so tight we had to leave everything in the car before entering the facility. We even had to remove our coat and shoes at the security check. Then we went through seven or eight secured iron doors as we approached a large group of prisoners singing on the lawn facing east and waiting for the sun to rise.

It was a beautiful sight, the prison choir in green robes and the prisoners singing at the top of their voices. It was a true joy to participate in a service to celebrate the resurrection of Jesus with those men. We met again with the men and their families at an 8:00 a.m. service, and Jeff gave a sermon which touched everyone present. Many accepted Christ that day, both in the prison yard and the auditorium with the families.

One thing is certain in this uncertain world, Jeff Park is still mining diamonds and finding hidden treasures even after P.T.L. is gone. C.O.P.E. (Coalition of Prison Evangelists) serves as a criminal justice ministry through uniting and networking ministries, training and equipping, providing resources and leading by the example of Matthew 25:36, "I was in prison and you visited me."

Reverend Frank Costantio, C.O.P.E. President, states in one of the organization's publications, *"We believe the Bible directs that the strong should serve the weak. As leaders, we should invest ourselves to provide encouragement and practical expertise to those God is calling to do His work."*

Now in the second decade, with an over 500 member ministry, C.O.P.E. is seeing an effective ministry multiply out of relating and serving one another. The ministries are cooperating to invest leadership in developing chaplaincy and prison ministries in Eastern Europe, the Caribbean, Europe, and Africa. It is a service organization, devoted to building fellowship, excellence, and unity among those God has called to a criminal justice ministry. The members serve, share resources, train, network, and help to keep each other on the cutting edge of effective criminal justice evangelism and discipleship. Recognizing that God uniquely calls ministries, C.O.P.E. does not dictate how each prison ministry under its umbrella should operate, but challenges members instead to ethical excellence, submission to God's ordained correctional leadership, and supportive interaction with all valid ministries and churches. The one standard that they all have in common is the principle that the strong should serve the weak.

More than 500 individual jail and prison ministries have joined C.O.P.E., growing in fellowship, encouragement, effectiveness, and professionalism. The C.O.P.E. Ministry Directory provides members with a complete list of chaplain names, addresses, and phone listings of every federal prison in the United States and Canada, cooperating churches, speakers and Aftercare listings. The C.O.P.E. quarterly newsletter keeps members abreast of happenings throughout the criminal justice system and ministry and fellowship opportunities throughout the world.

Al Lewis, Director of Covenant Prison Ministry once said, *"C.O.P.E. discipled me when I was in prison. Then when God called me into a ministry, they helped train my Board of Directors, provided free training for our Aftercare Ministry staff, held two successful fund-raising banquets and has been there for me when I needed the fellowship and support."*

Another testimony comes from Jim Spence, Director of the New England Aftercare Ministries in Holliston, MA. He states, *"C.O.P.E. has been a great source of enablement, encouragement and loving correction. I've learned ministry skills and how to wisely run the business end. C.O.P.E. brothers have loved me, sacrificed for me, strengthened me, and helped heal my wounds."*

Today, 18 prisons are being ministered to in the former Soviet Union. Seventeen prison chaplains have graduated, prison wardens have been saved, doors have been opened to place comprehensive Christian discipleship programs in those prisons. The Director of Prisons, a believer, told the press, *"These programs are the one thing that is improving the moral climate in our prisons."*

In the beginning, P.T.L. gathered a large group of churches and ministries which worked together. Today that is what C.O.P.E. is doing, gathering ministries to work together in the prisons.

A Letter From The Director

Deep within the soul and heart of every human being is the God given desire to be free. We at Freedom Ministries and Chaplaincies believe that an individual can only obtain true continuing freedom when he or she has a personal relationship with God through the Lord Jesus Christ

Freedom Ministries & Chaplaincies is privileged to serve and minister to those incarcerated throughout North and South Carolina. Whether a person is physically in jail or prison or locked up within himself, we are bringing wholeness, healing, and freedom to those with addictions to drugs, alcohol, gambling, criminal behavior and other life controlling problems.
We invite your support and involvement as we together reach out to our brothers and sisters providing encouragement, support, and the love of Jesus Christ.

Because of Calvary

Glenn Huelsman

FREEDOM MINISTRIES

At present, the Freedom Ministries and chaplaincies have approximately 100 dedicated volunteers throughout the Carolinas going into jails and prisons daily. They share and spread the Gospel through personal one-on-one evangelism and counseling, group Bible studies, weekend prison revivals and crusades and follow-up Bible Correspondence courses for discipleship and evangelism.

Sparklng diamonds from a few of the hundreds of letters from inmates who have been helped by this ministry follow:

"I used drugs and drank a lot. I'm not saying this to make an excuse on why I am here. It is just so you know where I'm coming from. I have a beautiful wife and two lovely children. I went to college and had very good professional jobs. I made lots of money but wasn't happy. I so desperately want to be a good husband and a great father to my children. My wife and children are Christians, and she was always trying to tell me about God, but I just wouldn't listen. It got me here doing this time and not able to see my wife and kids. What a waste! I hurt people who meant so much to me, but they still love me because they are Christians. I don't how to say or write this, but I accepted Christ today. I believe His Spirit is in me. Please pray for me and my family."

* * * * *

"I know God is with me. All I have to do is live by the Bible. I desperately want to be home with my family. I just hope I'm well enough to make it. I'm hoping that I can use this time I have left to better myself and to get to know God and let His plan for me reveal itself to me. You made a difference in my life. I hope I can someday thank you in person for helping to get my life back on track."

* * * * *

"I would like to thank you for being my personal hero. God is not asleep. I have five years to go until parole. I have a degree in _____, the Lord sent me here because I drifted away from Him and into drugs, sex, and alcohol. I always wanted to be a doctor. I've never been in prison before, and I don't want to see my family because they are ashamed of me for being here. But I love them."

* * * * *

"I was very happy to complete your Bible course. It was very helpful to me. I am a Babe in Christ. I have received God and Jesus His Son as my personal savior. Please pray for me and my children and all human beings who enter the jails."

* * * * *

"May the God of Abraham, Isaac and Jacob be with you always and forever. I thank our Lord and Savior Jesus Christ for the Word you bought on faith this past Sunday. And most important, that 39 men were saved. We're praying they continue on. When I get out, I want to work somewhere in the presence of the Lord or in a Christian environment and spirit. I feel the rest of my life will be on the Christian side of the system. I have been locked up for over twelve years, and I have nothing but Jesus and ministries like yours to depend on. I love the Lord. I find every day that I know so little about Him. I want to know and experience His Love to the fullness so I can go anywhere and stand for the Lord. I will never come back to the prisons except to fellowship with the Brothers in here. God bless you for all you do."

* * * * *

"I would just like to take time to send my appreciation to the Freedom Ministries family in trying to keep one strong in the Lord. I grew up in a "true Christian"

environment. When I came to prison, I lost contact with my family. I've been caught up in the struggle of trying to take care of myself and at the same time stay strong in God's work. Frustration and depression take their toll. I read my Bible and pray. I honestly want to get my life "right" and in one accord with the Lord. I know He is real."

* * * * *

"I am one of the people who participated in your marriage seminar. It was almost as if we had a normal life for a few days. The religious services were good ... and the talking about our thoughts and beliefs. Being able to use the free time to just sit and talk and be outside together was really nice."

DOGWOOD MANOR

Dogwood Manor is another "diamond" that was mined from P.T.L. It is a Christian Men's Discipleship Home where broken and battered lives are healed and gently restored to wholeness through God's love, discipline and encouragement. The rough diamonds are polished there every day and still shine brightly. Dogwood Manor began with P.T.L. building a center to house men just out of prison. The land across the railroad tracks from the hotel and the farm was used to build a place for 120 men.

The idea was to teach the men life skills. They had vocational training, spiritual foundation training, and disciplines. They taught them the basic responsibilities of manhood. Jeff Park says, *"it was a place for men to be reparented who had never had a dad to teach them the ways of life."* Unfortunately, when P.T.L. ended, the facility had to be closed. Some of the staff and clients went from there to another program called "Rebound" and Dogwood Manor was started to house six men.

Dogwood Manor is a nonprofit ministry operated through the leadership of the Coalition of Prison Evangelists and Freedom Ministries and Chaplaincy. It provides a healing recovery program. Modeled on Christian love, the program helps the participants build a personal devotional life with God, learn to love and respect others in community living, and develop work and social disciplines that free them from the enclavements of their past.

Residents must make a one year commitment (six months' residency and six months' reentry training). Upon entrance they obtain day employment, aided by a job developer. Three evenings a week, residents attend the Victorious Living Bible School by video (accredited Bible College courses that provide a Biblical foundation of understanding God's will, the Church, and victorious living in the world.) Residents graduate the one year program with a certificate and college credit.

Other facets of resident rehabilitation include the weekly overcomers class, counseling, church and individualized service strategy. Residents assist in writing their own recovery contract which is evaluated and revised every three months. Volunteers are needed to help with:

1. Tutors and monitors for video Bible School and Overcomers Groups.
2. Transportation for Video Bible School and Overcomers Groups.
3. Practical help in Home Operations (cooking, recreation, etc.)
4. Providing needs (furniture, utensils, etc.)
5. Praying faithfully for the home and residents.
6. Personal counseling and mentoring.
7. Financial support.

If you'd like to help, you can phone 803-548-2670. There are opportunities to minister, *Diamonds in the Rough*, all around us. All we have to do is search them out. Many of us know someone who needs help, a friend, a family member, maybe even ourselves. I pray that God will help us to have compassion for those around us and remember that He loves them just as He loves us. Jeff Park states *"that the goal of Dogwood Manor and the Prison Ministry is to build relationships with men and then disciple them through the Word of God and testimony to Christ."*

The following letter is from David Reimenschneider:

Dear Reader,

My knowledge of P.T.L. came from the television ministries. I had seen Jim and Tammy on the air and their message to me was trying to spread God's love. Their message was the prosperity that was promised in the Bible. So many people misunderstand that -- it tells us specifically in the Bible that we are to prosper as our soul prospers. And that message struck home with me.

At that particular time in my life I was certainly not involved in the church, but for some reason that caught my eye and I continued to listen. Seeds were planted -- I'm out here striving for all the things of the world and yet the happiness that Jim and Tammy talked about on tv, I didn't have, and I couldn't understand why. And the more I listened, the less peace and happiness I had in the lifestyle I was living. After the demise of the P.T.L. organization, there were a lot of things that went through my mind. Why do these things happen? Words came to my mind: Don't judge the message by the messenger and don't put your faith and trust in any one man. And over and over again, look at what is being done, not at who is doing it.

There was a lot in the newspaper and on television, concerning abuses, and it broke my heart because I was aware of the way things were being ridiculed by people who had no idea what they were talking about -- taking an incident and blowing it out of proportion. Christ died for us and we're all sinners, and yet we want to point fingers at those who fall, and we don't want to let them get back up. God uses every one of us. Take a look at Paul. We're supposed to be a Christian family, all members of one body with Christ as the head. And each member needs to be supported by the rest.

When I have a problem or a question, I go to the Bible. And the Bible tells me that there is a rejoicing in Heaven over the one who returns more so than 99 who are already there. I believe that the focus of the ministry to begin with at P.T.L. was trying to show people that there was a true joy in praising the Lord. That is our purpose here on earth to praise and glorify our Father in Heaven. Now a lot of things get twisted around. I have been fortunate in as much as the seeds that were planted continued to grow. I am thankful that some of those ministries that were originally started by P.T.L. have continued on, especially the prison ministry.

I was brought up in a very strict, religious family, spent three years in a Roman Catholic Seminary and left that in rebellion. After serving my time in the military, my life was a life of achieving. Whatever I was told I couldn't do, I was out to prove I could. I was blessed, although at the time I would never have admitted it, with great successes in the world. In 1992, I was involved in a company and was hurt on the job. Due to circumstances, the company refused to take care the injuries and I literally went out of my mind in anger and rage and ended up in prison. I served my time there in Florida and came to South Carolina where I was released in 1993. There were some chaplains there and I got involved in some of the educational programs. I picked my Bible up and started studying it again.

When I came to South Carolina, I associated myself with a small church and became your Sunday Christian, went to church on Sunday, Wednesday night and was out trying to earn a living and build a career. In December 1995, I was working with a company and we ran into some legal difficulties and I ended up in 1996 being charged with some things concerning the performance of my job. Legally it should have been a civil matter, but it was turned into a criminal matter and I ended up spending another 60 days in jail.

During that period of time there was a chaplain in the York County Detention Center who was part of Freedom Ministries, an offshoot from the original P.T.L. ministries. I met Jeff Park who is the President of Freedom Ministries. I was impressed with Jeff because at that time in my life I had realized where I had been -- that God was standing out there waiting for me to ask him to come in because I had thrown him out. I realized I had been spending my energies in the wrong way. It wasn't illegal or sinful, just wrong. When

I was released, I had heard about the reentry program of Freedom Ministries. One of the deacons at my church opened up his home to me, but the Holy Spirit said "You need to go to Dogwood Manor." I tossed and turned and the next morning talked to Jeff. I went through the program at Dogwood Manor. People came there having no idea what to do next. This was a place to take a babe in Christ and allow him to grow. It was a place to build a foundation. I began assisting Jeff with the computer system and programs. I realized then that this offshoot of P.T.L. was continuing where P.T.L. had left off. It was ongoing. Although the names had changed, the same people were involved, the same Holy Spirit, and the same ministry was there. The work was still going on. This man who had been instrumental with P.T.L. in prison ministry had overcome many hurtles and was still working for Christ.

Thelma Pointkowski lives next door to Dogwood Manor. She is a lady called by God into a special ministry. She tries to mentor the men, and is willing to help them in any way, from taking them to job interviews to cooking food or showing them how to do laundry or wash dishes. She's constantly in prayer for the men and the ministry.

In the year I've been associated with Dogwood Manor, there have been 25 men go through the home, and to my knowledge, every one of them is gainfully employed and in church now. The five or six members who are there now attend church. Everyone is working, and there are no ongoing problems with former addictions. Some of these guys had life controlling problems, workaholics who destroyed themselves and their families, gambling, overeating, sexual addictions, as well as drugs and alcohol. Through the program at Dogwood, there is no sigma to having an addiction. Number one is to realize we can't overcome this on our own. The power must come from God. That is the basis on which Dogwood exists. This is a sheltered environment which gives the individual time to take the necessary steps to go back into society.

Dogwood Manor gives the men a chance to get a foundation before going back into the world. My involvement with

Jeff continues. Because of having been in a prison and seeing what goes on, I am called personally to minister to the men in Mecklenburg County prisons through Freedom Ministries. My pastor is asking me now to head the Prison Ministry though our church in Columbia and over in Catawba County.

When my probation was violated, I had a fifteen years suspended sentence. I would go to jail for 10 years if I violated my probation. God's hand was on the Public defender that I had in Florida. She did some background investigation, determined that my original sentence was illegal, got together with the district attorney and the judge and they negotiated to the point where rather than go through all the necessary legal proceedings if I would admit to violating the probations, the judge would resentence me, drop the probation, drop the fifteen years suspended sentence, sentence me to two years in the department of corrections in Florida and give me credit for the previous time served, which meant that when I went in front of the judge I had 29 days left to serve.

I spent those 29 days in prison ministering to men, letting them know that there is something on the outside to go to. In the county facility while waiting, I maintained a Bible Study, preached two revivals, and a number of men came to Christ and many rededications. While at the state prison facility, again God's hand was on me. I had daily devotionals and just the sight of the Bible drew men and caused them to ask questions. I told them this was the only way of life. Because of that, I now correspond with eleven of them. Many of them are interested in Dogwood Manor and are looking for the joy and peace they saw reflected in others. They knew I wasn't a phony. We become transparent before the Lord.

With these men, you must be totally honest and have the gift of God's love in your heart. If you're trying to give that to them, they can feel it. I received a great revelation. I don't do anything for God. I don't do anything for Jesus. Everything I do is <u>with</u> God and <u>with</u> Jesus. There's a contemporary gospel group, the Williams Brothers, who have a *song out now that says, "I'm nobody that wants to tell everybody that there is somebody that can change anybody." That's the way I feel about myself and the way God is using me now.*

Satan will twist and turn and deceive. Sometimes when we get in a leadership position, we get our eyes off the true meaning of leadership and that leadership translates to service. When we quit serving, personal gain and praise step in, and we get in trouble. Today, too many people are serving <u>the God of what might be</u> or <u>the God of what could have been</u> instead of <u>the God that is</u>. Our God tells us we are not supposed to worry about yesterday or be concerned about tomorrow because the trials and temptations of today are sufficient in themselves. We have gotten away from God. Our money says, "In God we Trust," but we don't. We have lost our basic moral foundation which is outlined for us in the Bible.

I doubt if many people realize just how far reaching were the ministries of P.T.L. There were millions and millions of people that were touched. Most people only knew about the huge buildings and television programs. You never heard about the small people, the women in trouble, the prison ministry, those in need, the little houses that they set up to meet people's daily needs all over the country. There were so many things buried, but those are showing up now, and can be traced back to P.T.L. God continues to use these ministries and the people involved. We need to look forward and focus on the overall situation instead of the one man.

Each one of us has the most powerful tools, prayer and love. When you share love, barriers are dropped, honesty takes over, facades are dropped, and false fronts are done away with.

David Reimenschneider

NEW HOPE FELLOWSHIP

New Hope Fellowship was another Jewel in the making at P.T.L. In 1988, Jim Gray served as National Director of the New Hope Fellowship's 120 chapters across the country and at P.T.L. These organizations assist Christians in battling alcohol and drug addiction.

The fellowship meetings have a non-threatening, non-judgmental atmosphere, which give opportunities to share problems, fears, and hopes during the individual and/or group sessions.

In the meetings, New Hope leaders try to assist the individuals in developing a personal relationship with Christ and initiating a disciplined process of living out spiritually motivated principals, based on the Word of God, in family, work and church life.

Fort Hope was the home that P.T.L. built to help men get off drugs and alcohol. It was designed to bring them into a closer relationship with God, free them from destructive addictions and train and prepare them for a new life.

Mark was one of the first graduates from Fort Hope, and in the following letter he tells us his story.

Dear Reader,

Before I came to Fort Hope, my life was mainly made up of drinking and doing drugs all day long for seventeen years. Then one day, my friends and I were sitting around drinking in one of the friend's backyard when we noticed a full page ad in the newspaper. It was from a church and said "If you need to be set free from drugs or alcohol, we will help."

We decided to go, kind of joking around, but I was really sick of the way I was living and wanted to get out of it. It wasn't fun any more. So we went to this church, drunk; but people began hugging us. Older ladies, children, everyone was hugging me and I wasn't very huggable. My friend went up to the altar, and after a while I went up to see what was going on, and they began praying for me.

I felt something there I'd never felt before, a total peace, so I kept going back to the services. I was still a total mess, however. I'd leave the sanctuary half way through the service, chug down a couple of beers and come back in, and yet they kept loving me.

Finally I told them I needed to get away from my friends in Florida if I was going to quit. That was in 1986 and I was 29 years old. They found a place for me to stay in Fort Hope at P.T.L. I had never heard of P.T.L., but they told me I was leaving in about a week, and this man was going to drive me up there. I mixed a two liter bottle of vodka to see me through the drive up to P.T.L., and I about smoked the driver out of his truck.

I was surprised by Fort Hope. They didn't talk about alcohol. They talked about the Lord. I had never had withdrawal symptoms before, but I had never had a time when I ran out of liquor. I always managed some way to get more. So when I first went off it completely, I had the shakes really bad. I finally went down to the Upper Room and had this pastor pray for me. I was really thinking this isn't going to do any good, but when I walked out of there, I had stopped shaking.

God took the desire for alcohol and drugs away. I didn't know it until months later however. Maybe if I'd known I would have left, but instead I stayed there for a year. We had Bible study classes, seminars, and went to the preaching services. There were different activities during the day and work that we had to do. I worked at several different places and later received training in heating and air conditioning and went over to the hotel and volunteered for a while.

I had medical and dental care as well as a place to live while I was there. I was one of the first graduates from Fort Hope, and I'm doing well now. I have a good job, am married and have two children, and the Lord has been nudging me into going into street ministry.

A person has to reach the point where he or she wants help. You can't force it on anyone. When you get to the point where you are sick of the way you are living and you call out to the Lord, He'll find a way to help you. Fort Hope was the vehicle God used to help me. I have never missed anything from my former life, never had a reason to go back to it.

I had never had people to love me before. I had people that hung around me because I sold drugs, and deep inside, I knew if I didn't have anything for them, they wouldn't be there. They weren't friends. Today I have real friends. The people at Fort Hope and P.T.L. were real friends. I thank God for them.

After I'd been at Fort Hope, I went back to visit my church in Florida. I walked in expecting them to be all happy to see me, but they didn't even recognize me. I had changed so much -- in appearance -- in every way. I sat there in that church, a new creation, and couldn't even relate to the person I had been before. I went around and visited my old friends and sat with them where we used to drink every day. They were all drinking, and I tried to talk to them about God. I didn't want to be there, but I knew I was there to try to witness to them.

When I got out of Fort Hope and started working with Heritage, I got a loan and built a house. Most people tried to tell me I couldn't get a loan, because of my background. Naturally you would have thought I couldn't possibly have gotten a loan. But if God could bring me out of the mess I had been in, getting a loan was easy. I was really a different person. I knew everything about the person I had been before, but it was like that person wasn't me any longer. I truly was a new creation in God.

Mark Reeher

BRIDGE BUILDERS

Another ministry which has survived P.T.L. is that of the "Bridge Builders" organization. The leaders and members have been empowered by God to do a fantastic work, uncovering even more "diamonds in the rough."

This ministry is designed to help those millions of Americans who are imprisoned in compulsive behavior and/or self-destructive habits (such as overeating, gambling, TV watching, pornography, criminal behavior, and use of alcohol and/or drugs). Essentially all successful recovery programs, from such brokenness, contain a holistic, spiritual approach. Yet, few of these programs actually connect participants with the life-nurturing afforded in a local church.

"Bridge Builders" is a Church-centered and Christ-centered Discipleship program bridging Christians from brokenness to wholeness with the local church and equipping them to healing and wholeness. Their ministry philosophy is to afford a Christ-centered and biblically sound "journey out of the wilderness." The program is designed to promote the healing and development of healthy "family" and/or "church life."

The purpose of "Bridge Builders" is to facilitate regeneration, restoration and recovery, not just rehabilitation in individuals and ministries. They tell us that it is not a substitute for -- but makes personal humility and discipleship to Jesus Christ easier. The ministry provides a way to work the Biblical principles of 12 steps as they are applied to our vital connection to God, ourselves, and others.

There are two equally powerful parts to the "Bridge Builders" Discipleship program. The daily devotional called "The Way Home" where participants work through 12 Christian steps using prayer, journalizing and the study of God's Word.

The weekly "Bridge Builders" Support Group provides much needed accountability and encouragement through a short teaching time and small group discussions. This is a time when participants share thoughts, feelings and experiences with people of similar background and concerns. It creates a safe environment for them to open up and relate to each other. In "Bridge Builders," Christians integrate Scripture into their twelve step programs and share their spiritual background in the support group. The group focuses entirely on building a personal relationship with God and keeps religious doctrines at a minimum.

Ownership of each "Bridge Builders" Group is held not in the national organization, but in the local church and is participated in by the church leadership. This helps it to become a significant part of the life and ministry of the church. Bridge Builders are closed, committed groups consisting of two six-month journeys through the twelve steps. Participants who sign up must commit to working the daily devotional and faithfully attending the weekly support groups for six months. In the second six months, they have opportunities to become small group leaders. This prepares graduates to carry "Bridge Builders" outside the church to wherever God burdens their heart in a ministry.

The size of the group is from 12 to 30 people, with one fourth containing members who have completed the "Bridge Builders" 12 step program. If the group is beginning in a church, the four to six discussion leaders can be equipped by attending a Bridge Builder Leadership Seminar. Anyone who wants to experience the power of spiritual discipleship or become equipped to disciple others, can and should be a part of Bridge Builders. This would especially include those with self-defeating behaviors (and those who feel called to help those with these behaviors)which include: excessive use of drugs, alcohol, or food; overindulgence in sex, gambling, crime, spending or work; compulsive behavior expressed through constant volunteering, caretaking perfection or self-improvement; obsessive thinking about sin, weight, pornography, status or relationships; unreasonable aversion to crowds, evil spirits, rejection, sex, public speaking, or disapproval; and/or excessive attention and focus placed on others as a means of establishing identity and self-worth. A "Bridge has to be long enough to reach the other side," and "Bridge Builders" have been busy and are still very busy building those bridges.

For more information call 803-548-2670.

Chapter 5

GOLDEN GLITTERS

P.T.L. Centers

P.T.L. Centers provided free food, clothing, and spiritual help to the needy. They were one of the first outreach missions of P.T.L. Jeff Park and his wife were both very much involved in the P.T.L. Centers back then and today. He and his co-workers serve without stopping. The following is a personal letter from Jeff:

P.T.L. Centers - In 1981, Jim Bakker started PTL Centers providing free good clothing + spiritual help to the needy. Each of the 800 centers were placed in connection with a local church. So even though PTL folded, most continue to operate.

Let me share the story of just one. Shortly after we began this program, a widow from Charlotte, Barbara Benton, came to my office weeping, wanting to start a PTL Center. Her husband had been shot to death in the Double Oaks community and she was now burdened for this drug infested, violent (third most violent in US), neglected neighborhood. Even the police were afraid to enter so they had erected a ten foot high foot wide blocked long wall to separate the neighborhood from the huge public housing development next door.

Barbara wanted to start a Love Center in the middle of that violent center. Intrepidly we visited "Ways" Street to see houses boarded up and prostitutes and drug dealers openly pushing their "wares." Barbara convinced me to get the Heritage Church men + students involved and we brought the "pig picken" to offer free picnicing w/ Gospel music, food, and games for the children w/ prizes. Many folks, mostly unruly kids, would come out (rarely the child who won the race got the prize, but the kid who could grab + tear the prize from your hand)

Eventually, with Barbara (selling fried fish on the street), we were able to rent a place next to the park as a Love Center. PTL provided all the food & clothes for distribution. Soon there were 80 kids in a children's choir started. Prostitutes, drug addicts & whole families came for deliverance & salvation. Barbara began to march around the center next door with her followers every Sunday, claiming it for their own. The Center was where had been the First (black) Baptist Church until sold in '71. Now it housed prostitution downstairs & a pool hall (drug selling) upstairs. The Black Mafia wouldn't sell it to us until he became ill. Two days before his death, he sold the building to Barbara ((a sweet lady from PTL provided the money).

This church provided a "beachhead" for transforming the whole neighborhood. Guys coming to buy drugs were saved & put in Christian recovery & discipleship residential programs. Literacy programs for children & youth provided hope & encouragement. Gradually, the church grew to hundreds of members. The city of Charlotte saw such a transformation of the neighborhood that they partnered with Barbara (Genesis Park) to provide over a million dollars to restore the homes in the community. No longer were the police afraid to enter & they set up a satellite station in the neighborhood. Crack houses were bulldozed & new homes built with help from Habitat For Humanity. The community went from 3rd worst in the U.S. to the 41st worst in Charlotte. Such a change that the names of the streets (Kenny & Ways) were changed to Peaceful Blvd, Holy Spirit Hathaway, & Bewton Place in honor of the change.

Churches have gotten involved. My church has raised over $400,000 now to build a 1.5 million dollar multipurpose center to provide classrooms for literacy, a gym for recreation, & a sanctuary for the church.

All this happened because Jim started the PTL Center program & is just one story of the more than 800 centers established across America.

Jeffrey Park

In a recent interview, Jeff Park states, *"there were probably 800 People That Love Centers opened all over the country. I don't know what happened with all of them, but the one that was opened just outside the grounds was moved. We always intended for the Love Centers to be associated with local churches, so we moved that Center to Faith Assembly in Rock Hill. It is still operating there and people are won to Christ through that outreach every month.*

Many are still operating as outreaches of local churches. Another is operating really excitingly in Charlotte at the Community Outreach Church. We just raised $352,000 for the Church In the Inner City, the Community Outreach Mission. That has been the most exciting project that I've been involved with. This started in 1981 when Barbara Bruton came to the P.T.L. Center and was weeping that her husband had been shot to death there. It was a place where police were afraid to go in. The church had been turned over to the black mafia. It was such a violent community the city had directed that walls be built to separate it from the other homes. It was the third most violent community in America. There were deaths there every week and violence. She was preaching on the edge of the community in her brother-in-law's garage. The city was going to tear down the garage and build a parking lot, so she wanted us to help start a P.T.L. Center there.

We went into the area, brought the singers, played games with the kids, turned one of the buildings into a P.T.L. Center and in a couple of years, the church was taken back from the Mafia. A beautiful church was built, and the community has gone from the third worst violent community in the nation to the 41st worst in Charlotte. They have renamed all the streets to Peaceful Blvd., Holy Spirit Walkway. The whole community has been redone. There are other communities where the Body of Christ is getting involved. That is what works. Christians working hand in hand."

Uncle Henry and Aunt Susan Harrison

Chapter 6

SPLENDID SERVANTHOOD

Uncle Henry

When Margie and I first came to P.T.L., the one person that made the greatest impression on me was Henry Harrison, better known as "Uncle Henry." I had never met a more genuinely loveable person. There was no pretension -- just *"Hi there! Did you know that Jesus loves you?"* I remember sitting down at the dinner table next to Uncle Henry for the first time. He put his hand on my shoulder, grinned at me, and it was friendship on the spot.

He was the epitome of what P.T.L. stood for -- never a sour note during the bad times -- always cheerful. He was always forgiving and had something nice to say about others. Aunt Susan once said about her husband, *"I have watched this man I'm married to -- this man everybody calls Uncle Henry (and I call Honey), and I've tried to figure out how he can always be so loving. Now you might not realize that sometimes people treat Uncle Henry badly, or mistreat him, or hurt him emotionally. Yet these are the very things which have mellowed him and made him so sweet."*

"It's because he's been disciplined by some things that have hurt and still hurt deeply that he can be so loving. God has allowed these painful experiences, I'm sure, to create in him a compassion and a love for people who mistreat and despitefully use us. God says we've got to love them ... and I've watched Henry do this many times."

Uncle Henry & Ray Walters

Henry once told me, "I feel we are to live so closely to the source of love, God Himself, that it will radiate through us so as to affect every person with whom we come in contact -- a smile to the policeman directing traffic, a wave to the parking attendant, a pat on the shoulder and a joyous and sincere, 'God bless you,' to the person who draws our gasoline."

Uncle Henry brought glory to God by enriching the lives of many employees and visitors at P.T.L. He uncovered many hidden treasures in the people that God loved.

The following is a letter from Aunt Susan, wife and widow of our beloved Uncle Henry. She still lives on the grounds of Heritage today and ministers daily to friends and visitors.

Dear Reader,

Uncle Henry and I saw things that were "so right" with P.T.L, but only God knows the magnitude of all the far-reaching good around the globe. The two of us, however, experienced first-hand much good that will last through eternity. The so called "little things" in life many times have more impact than what we consider to be the profound ones.

For example, a very sad little man stood in a long line of those waiting to be immersed in water baptism by Uncle Henry at P.T.L. "Uncle Henry," he cried out, "the churches don't want me. I'm a street person!"

Uncle Henry asked, "Well, do you love Jesus?"

"Yes," he said, and Uncle Henry baptized him. Such unconditional love - Uncle Henry was no respecter of persons. His heart was so full of love. His smile and open arms greeted each one and they felt so loved! He loved with the true love of Jesus, unconditionally. He always loved, no matter how badly he was treated. The Bible says love those who persecute and despitefully use you. I think my husband came the nearest to that of any person I've ever known.

When we went to Hawaii to produce programs for the P.T.L. ministry, I realized some of the far-reaching and profound impacts the ministry was having. We'd learned that only between 1 and 2 percent of the residents there were Christians. My heart broke to see a God-given place so beautiful - like Paradise-lost!

I recall with great joy, even now, those powerful closing moments of the musical in the amphitheater. With Henry's shout giving the invitation to salvation, crowds rushed over to The Upper Room for prayer at the altar. It sounded like a trumpet blast resounding across the hills - welcoming them into The Fold! Only eternity will reveal the thousands of lives changed here on the P.T.L. grounds in Bible teaching seminars twice daily. The great audiences for the daily TV broadcast, camp meetings each night, and the Sunday services were all so powerful! There were marriage workshops, Inner Healing Seminars, Singles workshops, and more.

Words cannot describe the ongoing friendships of thousands whose hearts are joined in the precious love of Jesus forever who prayed for and nurtured hurting ones seeking answers.

Uncle Henry loved the home the Lord enabled him to design and build here. The two of us put our family inheritances together to support this project. Surely, in God's Plan for us, I am safe and loved and cared for since Uncle Henry winged his way to glory from this place he loved so much. God chose to put His name upon this Heritage USA property - and I say, so Be It!

Henry went to work for the Christian Broadcasting Network in 1967 and then went to the P.T.L. Club in 1975. I wish every person in the world could see the glory that he saw when he left this world. He had been getting weaker for quite some time. And up until the last five minutes of his life, I was praying that he would be healed here in this world. But his body was getting weaker and weaker. I left him sitting up in the bed with his chin on his chest fast asleep. I took our little dog out for a run and rushed back as quickly as I could for fear he might topple over while I was gone. I came back to the open door of the bedroom and saw something I had never seen before and doubt if I will again until it's my time to go.

The whole room was changed and his face was bright with color as it had ever been. His eyes were wide open and sparkling. He looked the way he had before he got sick. And he was shouting "Praise the Lord!" to the top of his lungs. I started to the bed and he said, "Jesus is my rock!"

I said, "You're better, You're better!"

He pointed up and said, "The presence, the presence, the presence!"

I gathered him in my arms and said, "Honey, how do you feel right now?" And he shouted, "Wonderful!"

There was the most joy I've ever heard in a voice in my life in his in that moment -- and then his spirit went into glory. I would never have called him back. I knew where he was, and I had gone as far as I could. I laid him in Jesus' arms, but I knew I couldn't stay. He had promised me for a long time that we were going together, and I know now that we did. I held his body in my arms and watched him go into Glory. Weeks after that, when I got still enough to hear that still small voice, God told me, "You did," and joy filled my soul.

I speak to women today, who have lost their mate. I speak to groups. God is using me to reach out to others and share this story. I am a part of Heritage community, I counsel on the phone and open my home for church and Bible studies.

Aunt Susan

Chapter 7

WINNING WEALTH

Telephone Ministry

The following letter is from Lou and Shelvie Hostetler and tells of when Shelvie and her husband Lou came to P.T.L.

Dear Reader,
We came from Ohio back in 1976. Lou had lost his job of twelve years. We weren't sure what God wanted us to do, but He opened up the door for Lou to go to a School of Ministry down in Bradenton, Florida. We came down here looking for a job, but God's timing wasn't right yet. We were down here for a few days, and while here tried to find people we had seen up in Canton, Ohio. We couldn't find the people we wanted to talk to, so we went back home distraught. We didn't know at the time that God had a whole different plan for our lives.
Then in 1977, I was working part-time, and Lou still hadn't found work, but God was still meeting our needs. So we came back for a visit to P.T.L. when they were in the studio on Park Road. It was on a Sunday afternoon. We went to a hotel over on Park Road, and we decided to go over to the grounds and look around. You could just feel the presence of the Lord. It was so peaceful. We had our four-year-old daughter with us and were walking around the studio building, not knowing that anyone

was around. When we got over to one side, Uncle Henry and Aunt Susan came down the stairs. We started talking and sharing, and they said that God had told them to take a break from their radio program and just go out and take a walk. And that's when we ran into them.

They invited us back upstairs to be on their radio program to share what God had been doing in our lives. So for about a half hour we shared what God had been doing, and then they invited us home to supper. Lou and Uncle Henry went to buy steaks, and Aunt Susan and I went on home to get things started. We had a very good meal and then looked at slides that they had from Israel. We stayed there until about 11:30 that night having a good time.

The next morning, we got up early and came into the studio where they were getting ready to do the program. One of the workers recognized us from telethons we'd done with them in Canton on the different occasions they'd been up there. They asked us to go to Personnel, because they knew there were some job openings. We filled out applications and they asked if we could be at work the following Monday. We just looked at each other. We were from Ohio, and they wanted us on Monday.

We found a place to live on Tuesday, paid a deposit, left and drove home in the middle of the night to pack. The man we rented our house from up there was a Christian man, and he said he knew when we left we weren't coming back. "You don't have to give me a notice or anything," he said. "Go with my blessing."

On Thursday, we arranged for our utilities to be shut off Friday after we left. A friend helped load us up. We were on the road Friday, back down here over the weekend, unloaded, in an apartment and Shelvie went to work on Monday. Everything was happening so fast, we didn't have time to think about it. We were so excited. We both have large families, and they accepted what we were doing. God had already gotten their hearts ready. We were just praising the Lord. God had planned it all.

He had everything timed. We couldn't have done it on our own.

We had never been away from home. Lou was a little Mennonite boy from Amish country and I was a homebody person. Our families were real close to us. We didn't want to leave them, but God placed it in our hearts to let go and that he would take care of us. And he placed it in their hearts to let us go. The night before we left, we realized it was God, because our daughter had not been sick at all. And all of a sudden that night, she got a severe earache. We had some friends of ours to pray over the phone and we laid hands on her and within a short time, she was better. We weren't going to let Satan have his way in it. We knew God had opened the doors and we were going.

When we got down here, we thought Lou had a job. God knows that Lou has a hard time accepting things in faith, so there had to be a job that looked like it was there for us to come back down here. But that fell through. So Lou had no job, but God had plans for him. I went to work. Teresa went to the day care center, and he went to work on the phones volunteering. God spoke to Lou's heart and said to work the telephones, that was where he needed to be.

Lou says, "You couldn't have pulled me off. The presence of God was there day and night. And the counselors got more of a blessing than the person we were praying for. We felt that God was in it all. I stayed on the phones for four months. I was happy there. It got to the point to where people brought loads of groceries there to where she worked and I put them in the car and took them home. All kinds of miracles happened to keep us going. We were never in total need. He let us get there to let us grow. He was in everything we did. This was the first time that I ever recognized this. I was raised as a Mennonite boy with a very good upbringing. But we didn't know God was as big or as personal as He really is, and I found that out by experience. As this happened, and I stayed on the phones, one day they asked me if I'd be afternoon Supervisor. So I graciously accepted that position. I wasn't there three months until they asked me to be part of the management, to do statistics and to start training people. This was in 1978. I trained thousands of people from then until 1990 for the telephones.

We were building a base for the phone volunteers. There were over 400 volunteering to work on the phones, some an hour, some a day, some one day, some four days, but a total of over 400 people. There were times that the sixty phones weren't quite fully manned. So I started to go to the audiences and ask for people ahead of time. We would train them quickly, and then train them more fully the next day, if they stayed. Many of them ended up on staff.

After a year or a year and a half, I could go to the audience and pick out a pastor. I'd say, "You're a pastor. Come on. Help us on the phones." One day, Bob Dearborn was sitting in the audience and I pointed right to him and his wife and said, "You're pastors. Could you help us on the phones?"

They said, yes, and we gave them a quick training and that day Bob Dearborn won more people to Christ than he had seen come to the altar in his church for six months or longer. They got so excited. They made good phone workers, so they were hired as staff on the telephones in the afternoons. He was then hired as a pastor and she as a pastor-follow-up on the grounds and in the Upper Room.

But that was just one story of how people were blessed by working the phones. Many, many people were blessed. A lot of people would hesitate at first, but I'd tell them we'd help them. Feel at home, relax, and let the Holy Spirit do the work. And the Holy Spirit always came through. Souls were won to the Lord through them. So many people came back and thanked me for coming to them and prodding them to go on the phones. Many would come down several times a year to visit and work on the phones while they were there. It blessed me to know that God would use a little farm boy in that manner. It was nothing I did -- I didn't even have the ability to speak, but I taught all those classes.

Everyone, who came to the Lord through the phones, was asked if they wanted a pastor to visit them. Many of them did or they at least wanted the name of a church in their area. We had hundreds and hundreds of people all over ready through our follow-up department to call on those people. They weren't left out on a string. Many didn't understand that these people who were won to the Lord were followed-up. One pastor told me that he had a pew full of a family in his church through one of them giving their heart to the Lord on the telephone. We will never know how that multiplied. I have heard so many stories of one person multiplying to other family members and over and over again.

One man who called had taken an overdose and realized after they'd called in that they didn't really want to die and wanted a counselor. The worker turned it over to me. Meantime, we had gotten in touch with a pastor in that area while we were talking to that person on the phone. That pastor was on the other end getting emergency people calling them and telling them the situation. We got an address. We worked on this end, the pastor on the other end. While we were on the phone, we heard sirens of the emergency people as they drove up. We heard the door being broken down and then one of their rescue people came to the phone and said, "We've got him. Everything's O.K. We'll take it from here."

That was one of many situations where God combined the people on this end and the people on the other end. Lou remembers once where a man had a gun to his head, and on the program, out of the blue, Jim pointed to the camera and said, "You out there who wants to take your life, don't do it." The man saw it and heard it on television and put the gun aside and called. We got a pastor to him within minutes. The pastor just lived around the corner and went to the man and got him saved and in a church. This is the way the program worked with the phones. The phones were the lifelines of P.T.L..

That was the whole purpose of Jim Bakker being on television. God put it together.

I remember in 1986 when Mike Adkins sang the song "Adoration," and he started ministering in the spirit. We had over one hundred phones, and even though the phone number wasn't even on the screen, the phones rang straight through, all day and all night even after the program was over. Those were the most calls we'd ever had. The song went into tongues. It was the first time anyone ever sang on television in prayer language. The spirit of God moved on people. As soon as one put the phone down, it would ring again. Jim started ministering. He told the television audience that they needed to know the Lord personally. From that one altar call in that one day, we had the most salvations we'd ever had. We had over <u>one thousand salvations in that one day.</u> And when the program was rebroadcast, there were more.

We want to tell people if God is speaking to you, don't hesitate. Do what He says. You can go next door. You can use your own phone. The world can be won, if it's done right. Work with a pastor. That's what it's all about. Looking back and reflecting, it's exciting to see all those people who were volunteering and working the telephones, how obedient they were. People were fearful when they started with the phones. I was the same way. But when I started teaching these people, God used it in a way that as soon as I started talking to them, they would relax. "You made it sound like we could do it," they said. I knew that wasn't me speaking. It was the Holy Spirit, and it would surprise me.

We had signs that said, "If you want to work the phones, come to the lower level of the Upper Room, and you'll be trained." The first day, Colonel Weston came. He didn't say he was the most decorated man in the United States. He just wanted to do something for the Lord. I taught him and he went on the phones. One day his wife came in and told me who he was, and I couldn't fathom it. He was the humblest man I'd ever seen. He touched lives and he's still touching lives.

The phones were supposed to ring in sequence, but sometimes they wouldn't. All of a sudden, one would ring way up on 55, and we'd think why did it ring up there? And then it would ring down here again. When we'd ask that person later, the person would say "Yes, that person was going through something that I've gone through." It was like God placed the calls to the right person so they could minister to them. We saw this happen hundreds and hundreds of times. Maybe someone had gone through abortion, and people who needed that kind of help would reach them on the phone. People need to know that God orchestrated the whole thing. This thing wasn't man made. That's where some of the public have a wrong view of what P.T.L. was all about. It was different from the view that the media gave. There were twenty-five thousand people here one time, and I was the sixth to the last person to go when everything was shutting down. There are so many people out there who say, "I wouldn't have that money back. I would have given it anyway." There are many people who came, who still come, who didn't care about the money. They cared about the healings, the people saved, and all the good that happened. One lady walked out of her wheel chair at home, came down here and told her story, and then worked the phones. "I can't ever repay what happened," she said.

I really believe that many people who were touched are pastors now, missionaries, teachers, or ministers. We'll never know how many were saved, and how many were saved through those who were saved. It goes on today because a fire was lit under these people. They are the hidden treasures. A lot of people never knew that the people were followed up. Many stories came in from the pastors who were blessed because they'd gone to see some of the people who were touched through the telephones.

Shelvie says, "I first worked in cashiers and then in prayer phones as a prayer phone worker. Counseling was done by the follow up pastors. The prayer phone workers were there to talk, or laugh or cry with people, what-

ever they needed. Then I worked as a liaison between the volunteers and the staff and later Lou and I both worked in statistics before I went to work in P.T.L. Enterprises."

Lou says, "To sum it all up, only God could do something like P.T.L. and what happened. Only God could put something like that together. It was so huge we will never know the impact on the United States and other countries. God brought us here. He brought the workers to work on the phones. And I'd like to let the world know that God was in everything that was done in spite of what happened. When the bad started happening, we ministered on the phones, we weren't there to explain or answer questions. We were there to help people. God is faithful. From the time that I went to school, all the way through, and even to this present day in my life, He is faithful, every day, every hour of every minute."

They both say I know that God was faithful to us and through us. We wouldn't take anything for the time we spent there. We had some hard times and some good times, but even in the hard times, we have seen God work in our lives. We have seen Him meet our needs. We are like a stone wall being built. Some of those stones aren't going to fit, and have to be ground down to fit. That's what God was doing in our lives, grinding us down so we all fit perfectly together to make that solid wall. I believe He called everyone who was here.

There are thousands of people out there who were touched by P.T.L. that are continuing to go on, continuing to serve God, continuing to touch people. It is a snowball effect, with more and more people being saved, this family touches this family, this neighbor touches this neighbor. It is not dead. It is going on, and it is going to go on for generation after generation. The ministries are continuing everywhere in other Christian organizations, in secular organizations, making a difference. Everyone is so happy and blessed to have worked here and been a part of God's work.

Lou and Shelvie Hostetler

This next letter is from Lester Traas:

Dear Reader,
We came to P.T.L. February 20, 1985. We had never attended the program before, and on our second day, they asked for telephone counselors. I volunteered and enjoyed the work so much that I continued for a long time from 3:00 a.m. to 12:00 noon when the program was over.

One day a young man called. He was divorced and lonesome. His name was John, and we're still friends today. He says that he was encouraged by talking to us. Now he is a happily married Christian man with a child. We call each other quite often and he says that he'll never forget how he felt and how much the telephone ministry helped to change his life.

My son, Louis and I would be at church on Sundays at 6:00 to set things up for the service and many times people would come in to pray for the service. My son would pray over each chair and encourage other P.T.L. members to come in and pray over those twenty-three hundred chairs. My first wife sang in the choir. She had cancer, and one night she was really sick when she went to choir practice. Before she left the whole choir gathered around her and prayed for her. P.T.L. people loved each other.

Those of us who worked on the phones would hold hands and pray for the sick at P.T.L. Sometimes we would bring food and have dinner after the P.T.L. program.
Lester Traas

The following letter is from Dora Traylor, another who helped to answer the phone calls that came in from television viewers. She was on Telephone #1 which meant that when a call came through, she would get the first call. Dora became a "Diamond in the Rough" while ministering in her special calling at P.T.L., and is still mining jewels Monday through Friday on the telephone for another Christian group.

Dear Reader,
I worked for the Munsing Wear Textile Corporation for

43 years of my life, and 35 years of that time I was on the road starting all their branch plants. Most of that time, I lived in motels. And every morning when I was getting ready for work, I would turn on the television at 5:00 ... and there would be this young man preaching. It seemed that no matter which state I was in, there he would be.

After listening to him several times, I finally stopped long enough to hear what he had to say and where this program was coming from. Being a backslider, I was very touched by what he had to say. The Holy Spirit was really dealing with me.

And then one day in Tennessee in yet another motel room, I turned the television on and there he was again. I started crying and told the Lord if He would find me a quiet place to retire, I would serve Him the rest of my life. I was getting close to my retirement years at that time. Several months went by and I had just returned to Minneapolis, MN, and was ready to go on vacation. I hadn't made any plans yet about where to go, so I went to the travel agency in St. Anthony Village and made reservation to go to Alaska. I had no more than come out of the travel agency when a voice on the right side of me said, "You don't need to go to Alaska. You need to go to P.T.L. and get your life straightened out!" Well, I was so surprised at this reprimand that I immediately turned around and went back into the travel agency and canceled my reservation to Alaska. Then I went home and called US Air and made a reservation to go to P.T.L.

When I arrived in Charlotte, North Carolina, I went to the car rental booth and inquired of the lady how to get to P.T.L. "I'm going there on vacation," I told her."

"You came here for a vacation?" she asked incredulously. "But there's nothing here in Charlotte to see."

"Oh yes, there is," I told her. "The P.T.L. Club at Heritage, U.S.A.!" She didn't know where it was, but another lady who overheard us talking directed me as to where to go.

I found Heritage, U.S.A. with no problem and was very impressed with what I saw. I tried to get a room on the grounds, but everything was full. Even all the motels around the area were full. So the desk clerk directed me to Rock Hill which was about eight miles from Heritage, and I stayed there for two weeks. I was so hungry for the Word of God that I attended every Seminar and service and loved every moment of being with the family of God once again.

This was in July of 1980, and Munsing had purchased another plant in Fairmont, North Carolina, which was not a long distance from Heritage, U.S.A. I was assigned to go there and start that plant, so on weekends I was able to go back to Heritage and enjoy the Christian fellowship.

In 1981, I went back for my vacation and that's when I really recommitted my life back to the Lord. I was baptized in one of the pools by Uncle Henry Harrison who was the anchor man for the P.T.L. television program. At that time, they had started building condominiums on the grounds, so I put a down payment on a condo and in July 1982, moved into my nice, quiet safe home at Heritage - the one I had prayed for in the motel in Tennessee three years previously when I'd promised the Lord I'd serve Him the rest of my life.

I remembered the promise, but I didn't know how I was going to serve Him. However as I watched the program on television, my attention was invited to the Prayer Line and the lovely lady in charge named "Judy Chavez." "I'm going to do what she does," I said to myself. So I went on the prayer phones in September of 1982 in the studio during the P.T.L. program and in the Upper Room during the times that P.T.L. was going strong.

While working on the phones one day, a man called from New York, and said to me, "You need to tell the guy who spoke in Jewish yesterday on your P.T.L. program that he'd better learn the Jewish language a little better than he spoke it yesterday," he said.

"That was Uncle Henry Harrison, the anchor man at the P.T.L. program," I said, "and he was speaking in tongues."

"I don't know what you call it, Lady," he said, "but he spoke in Jewish and I understood him." What a blessing that was to that man!

Another time when Jeff Park was our manager in the

Upper Room, he asked me if I'd be willing to be interviewed by him on the P.T.L. program. He wanted me to tell how I'd come back to the Lord through P.T.L. after backsliding. I agreed to be interviewed, and afterward, many people who were backsliders called and told how they came back to the Lord because they had listened to that program.

Another time, a lady called for prayer. She was going through a divorce, was devastated, and needed a job. It just so happened that she lived close to Heritage USA. She came to P.T.L., got a job in the real estate office, and later I had a chance to meet her. She couldn't thank me enough for directing her to P.T.L., because she was so happy with her job and what God was doing through her life.

Many suicidal people called and we were able to help them get counseling and help. P.T.L. helped many hurting people during their years at Heritage USA. The Unwed Mothers Home took in pregnant girls. Fort Hope took in men who were on drugs and alcohol and helped to rehabilitate them to a good life with the Lord.

Even after they closed down, I continued the work. I went to C.B.N. in Charlotte until they moved out of Charlotte, and I'm still on the prayer phones today for Morris Ceruello Ministry. The calls are diverted to my home in Heritage U.S.A. from the Charlotte studios. So, I'm still serving the Lord and have been for fifteen years. I thank God that the Holy Spirit never left me - even when I was a backslider - and that He led me to Heritage, U.S.A., to the P.T.L. Club where I came back to the Lord through the preaching of a young man named Jimmy Bakker. I believe God used Jimmy Bakker to bring me back to Him.

And I'm only one of many, many people who came to P.T.L. and were either saved or came back to the Lord through the ministries there. So many good things took place, and many happy memories are left with us who still live at Heritage U.S.A. I'm writing this to give glory to the Lord for His guidance and direction to the P.T.L. ministry and what it has meant to my life.

Mrs. Dora Traylor
Fort Mills, S.C.

Chapter 8

GLEAMING GIFTS

Radio and Television Ministries

The following letter is from Joyce and Bob Coleman in Murfreesboro, Tennessee and relates their experiences as a result of watching the television program.

Dear Reader,

It was December of 1993 when my husband Bob and I decided to take a flight to P.T.L. one weekend to see exactly what was happening. I had watched the P.T.L. television program and enjoyed it very much. I thought that a visit there during Christmas would be a nice Christmas present for both of us. Our children were now married and would be with their own children during Christmas, so we boarded our flight for an unforgettable trip to P.T.L. A glorious spirit-filled weekend was in waiting.

The bus from P.T.L. picked us up at the airport. As we entered the grounds, I knew immediately there was something different and very special for me. I wept so much that weekend that my husband was kept busy giving me tissues. I wasn't weeping because of sorrow or sadness, but weeping for joy.

The first night we all loaded on the tram and sang Christmas carols to the top of our voices on our way to the

Barn to see *"the Christmas Story."* The lights were glowing beautifully as our tram rounded the curves, and our voices rang out with carols of the birth of our Savior, Jesus Christ, God's only Son. We were singing from the heart, and everyone was feeling the joy of this special season.

The following day, we attended services, all filled with the presence of the Holy Spirit. I cried and cried. Never had I shed so many tears. It was a joyous occasion and made me wonder where I had been all my life. I had never been around so many people who so openly loved the Lord and spoke so freely about what God had done in their lives. I had been brought up in Church. My parents were Christians. They loved the Lord, but I had never felt so much love in my entire life.

When time came to leave, needless to say, I didn't want to go. But I knew I was leaving with something special, something that I did not have when I came. "I had met Jesus. He was now my savior. He would be with me forever. No one could take Him away." I felt a cleansing in my body, a cleansing as if the Lord had reached down from His throne and washed away every sin, every hurt that I had suffered. I had been washed in the Blood of the Lamb. I had a new life in Him.

On another occasion, my husband and I were leaving for a weekend flight to P.T.L, when He hurt a muscle in his back while taking a shower. He had suffered with his back many times in the past, so this was not the first time. When we arrived at P.T.L., we went to the cafeteria for lunch. A very sweet young lady came to our table to take our order. "How are you today?" she asked.

"O.K.," I said, "but my husband does have a back problem." She laid her hand on his back and prayed. And as we left the cafeteria, I noticed my husband was walking straight. "Look," I said, "you are not bent to one side as you usually are with your back problem." To this day, he has not had any further back problems. My husband is a physician, and we laughingly say now, that God even heals physicians. We give glory to God.

Another time I had a wonderful experience while staying at our Time Share after the grounds were closed to the public (we have been on the grounds every year since 1983 at least once). I had walked down to the Upper Room. I couldn't enter, but I was standing on the hill above it. There was no one in the area but me, and I heard a beautiful angelic choir, singing so beautifully that I cannot describe it.
Joyce and Dr. Bob Coleman

This letter is from Ed Anderson in Brampton Ontario, Canada. He sent it to us when he heard that we were putting together a book about the good aspects of P.T.L. "We hear so many negatives about religious organizations today," he said, "that it does become depressing. But God is good and 'His faithfulness endureth to all generations,' so I am most anxious to let you know of the good things that happened to me way back in 1981."

Dear Reader,
I was brought up in a religious Pentecostal family, and my parents instilled in my life, the Word of God to the best of their ability. They trained me up in the things of the Lord, even thought I personally did not believe or accept it. Yet the seeds of God's Word stayed with me.
One night back in 1981, at 11:30 p.m., I was watching P.T.L. while Jim was preaching the Word. When he finished preaching, he pointed his finger at the camera and asked, "If you died tonight, where would you spend eternity?" I felt like he was pointing directly at me, and I knew if I died that night, I would spend eternity in hell. I knew that I was a sinner. I was convicted in my spirit to make things right with God through his Son Jesus Christ.
I repented that night, was saved, born again, and have been serving the Lord ever since. Prior to watching the television program that night and giving my life to the Lord, my marriage was in trouble and going down hill. My drinking and gambling were taking a toll on our lives together. Our marriage was renewed that night, and our lives to-

gether have not been better or more blessed of God.

I cannot even begin to tell you of all the really wonderful things that God is doing in our lives today. I can only praise His Holy Name!

Ed Anderson

Dear Reader,

Almost fifteen years ago while I was in the Upper Room, the Lord impressed upon my heart these words: "I have KNIT your heart to this place for a reason". I'm not sure if I yet know THE reason, but I know many reasons why He let me be so involved in Heritage USA and its many facets.

The Lord used PTL and Heritage USA to mature me, a rather sheltered individual, by allowing me to experience so many new things. I remember the day I spent five hours on the prayer phones, one of those hours on the TV show. While the camera was on me, my phone lit up. I picked it up and a lady in Seattle said, "You have on a yellow blouse, don't you?" Oh my, it was then that I really understood the dynamics and impact of Christian TV.

I marvelled how one ministry could reach out into so many different areas:

>The Girl's Home for unwed mothers/adoption placement.

>Fort Hope for men freshly out of prison to learn a new skill, live together and grow in their faith.

>The People That Love Centers supplying basic needs to hurting people.

>Homes where people could come to live permanently. One section had a living arrangement for folks with special needs - a common living area surrounded by private rooms.

>An amphitheater where an incredible Passion Play was presented each summer.

>Outstanding Teachers and Preachers regularly teaching in buildings throughout the grounds, often shown on the TV network as well.

>The Upper Room open for prayer 24 hours a day everyday, as were the prayer phones.

>The Campgrounds, the Heritage Inn, the Lodges, and the Heritage Grand Hotel there for people to come for a wholesome vacation as well as ministry. Believers came by the thousands, but you know, non-believers came too, found acceptance, help, and many found the Lord.

The grounds and flowers at Heritage USA were so beautiful, and the buildings all beautifully decorated. All these things were prototypes of what the Church, the Body of Christ, could and should be doing. Heritage USA inspired possibility thinking for ministry.

Once upon a time I brought a bus Tour Group down from Cincinnati. We all stayed together in one of the big double Lodges. What fun! And what a responsibility. Looking back, I can hardly believe I did that.

A number of the PTL staff have become close friends with my husband and me, particularly Dick and June Hall and Michael Miller. There are many others who we have gotten to know too. Such special people! We have all shared together in the joys and sorrows that came as a result of PTL. That really KNITS you together.

My husband Keith and I have been to Heritage USA every single year since we discovered this incredible place. (Thank you Larry) Many of you will remember that the whole park was closed for some time after Hurricane Hugo. But God opened a door. At the last possible moment, a trustee gave permission and we were able to spend a week in one of the Time Shares. Hugo had done quite a number! Evergreens were at 45 degree angles, huge trees in the woods and campgrounds were down, much wreckage was apparent. We could look across Lake Heritage, from the lovely Time Share, at the Grand Hotel standing idle and somewhat damaged. Sad? Yes sad. But as I took daily walks around fallen trees and through the woods and recreation areas that I knew so well, I prayed. I thanked God for all the good that had happened there. I asked God's forgiveness for the sin that had occurred there. Then I prayed something unusual. I asked for God to forgive "this place". Then I asked the Lord to restore it according to His will. Now you can see how much I am "KNIT to this place".

Keith and I attend the Heritage Reunions each Labor Day weekend. How glad we are that Sam Johnson brings the remnant together. So if by chance your heart was "KNIT to this place" too, come and join us next year.

Ann Kintner

The next letter is from Hazel Higgins.

Dear Reader,

One day I was in the kitchen when I heard my husband cry out, "Hazel! Hazel! Come here."

I ran in to see what he wanted. He was in the living room turning the channels on the television and had come across a man in a river baptizing a lot of people. There were big trees on the banks of the river that looked like they used to years and years ago. The man was Jim Bakker, but we had never heard of him. All we knew was that we enjoyed watching him baptize all those people the old-fashioned way.

Later on, we saw him again on television and found out that he had bought some land on Park Street and was remodeling a big old house to use in his ministry. Of course, in the future, Jim bought land at Heritage, U.S.A. in Fort Mill, South Carolina.

Before my husband died, we continued to watch the television programs, and sometimes I would look up and tears would be running down his face. We got so many blessings out of the show. It was a real joy to watch what God was doing and had already done. The first time I walked into Grand Hotel, I felt like shouting. It was so beautiful! I thought of Solomon's Temple. I had never seen a place like that before where everyone liked to talk about Jesus.

When we look at P.T.L. today, we must look at how many souls were saved. One soul is worth the whole world. I still go to Heritage USA and have every year since it started. This year the Time-Share people got together several times and had a wonderful time together. We went to Aunt Susan's and Mr. and Mrs. Kent Hubbard's for services and worship. The Lord is still there. God forgives us when we make mistakes and remembers them no more. Thank God He does, and we must do the same.

Mrs. Hazel Higgins

The following letter is from Ron Aldridge in Ft. Mill, S.C.

Dear Reader,

I was a Minister of Music in a church in Florida and would go out occasionally to sing in other churches. The church there supported me in my traveling ministry as well as my local ministry. One time I was singing a cantata for a church. Larry Brubaker was on leave of absence at the time from the P.T.L. orchestra, and he was playing in the band at the church in Orlando.

When he went back to P.T.L., Ed Wheeler, the leader of the music department, said he needed a baritone, and Larry said he knew a guy he should call. The night before they called, my wife and I were driving around, and I asked her, "if you could live anywhere in the United States, where would you live?" She said she'd like to live closer to Virginia. I told her I'd like to live in that area too. The next morning I received a call from Larry Brubaker at P.T.L. saying they were looking for a baritone. My "pat answer" was "I'm very happy where I am." The church was very good to me. I was an Associate Pastor and responsible for a small section of the church. We had 65 people in our home every Wednesday. It was a very successful ministry and the Lord was blessing. I was getting ready to give him my pat answer, but the Lord checked me and I said instead, "I'll consider it."

I had written some songs and choruses earlier in my life, but as soon as I hung up the phone I went to the piano and wrote, "Let's Fill This House With Praise." The creativity started to flow out of me again at that point. I realized that I had been a little stifled creatively. To me, that was confirmation that I was to go. So we came up to P.T.L. and worked through the agony of working at P.T.L. I was told before I came, you go to work at 8:00, have a devotional, sound checks at 8:30, then go to the dressing room, get dressed, put on your makeup, come up, do the show, be done with the show at 12:00, eat a snack, come back at 1:00, practice till 3:00, and you're done. In reality, my schedule was to get there at 8:00 and work through a dinner theater. I would go to work on Monday and get home in time to see my kids for about two hours before they went to bed.

Our youngest was eleven days old when we came to P.T.L. in February of 1985. I would leave work Tuesday morning, kissing my children before I left for work, then work until 10:30 or 11:00 at night. We had to do a brand new song every day for "Tammy's House Party" according to the theme for that day. Most days I would write the song or rewrite an older song while the others were at lunch. I loved it, and it was a great opportunity, but it was too much. I was too exhausted to even go to church on Wednesday night. On Thursday, I wouldn't even see my children until Friday evening. Through all this, however, I knew that an effective ministry was going on.

I remember going to the show one day, a normal day with a normal format and normal guests. This was 1988, and I was hosting. It was one of those times when we were getting ready to move into something else. Something caught my heart, and I began to share. I didn't know what I was going to say, but I knew I needed to take some time for a personal ministry, to be more intimate. So I began to minister to hopeless people. And during this time of ministry, I said, "You may be completely destitute, completely hopeless, not even know what you're going to do with the rest of the day -- you may be sitting there with a gun in your lap and trying to muster the courage to kill yourself. But you have to understand -- there is hope."

Probably two years after I left P.T.L., I got a phone call. I was in a hurry to go somewhere, but the woman told my wife what had happened. So I put Deb on the phone and they talked for a long time. She said, "I was standing here doing the dishes and I thought of your husband and the effect that God had on my life through him. I was sitting there watching the program with my husband's gun in my lap, and I was going to kill myself. I had agriphobia. I couldn't go out of the house. My kids were very young. I couldn't even go to the grocery store without absolute fear. Your husband spoke right to me, and because of that, I didn't kill myself. I'm standing here now, doing my dishes, watching my kids play in the yard, and if it had not been for his obedience that day, I wouldn't be here enjoying my kids."

My flesh was saying you're working too hard, but I was at P.T.L. under the leadership of the Lord. I knew that I was called of the Lord to be there, and I knew I had to do what I was asked to do by those in authority. Once I got a letter from a man in South America. Someone had sent them a tape of the program. I read the letter to the other singers, and we were all fascinated by the way the man had been touched by God through that tape.

I'm just boggled by the multiplicity of the world of television. That's why I'm still in Christian television. You never know whom you reach. Music is a great tool of encouragement, of worship, and of building up the body.

After Jim left the ministry and while Reverend George was still there, they were having a fund-raising weekend. The singers were there singing on Main Street. Everything was fine. I looked up and saw three older ladies and I wondered about them. Then I saw a mother and two children walking down the street together. It was like a brick fell from Heaven and hit me on the head. I borrowed a pencil from one person and a piece of paper from another, and I sat there and wrote the entire song, "There Is An Answer" in the middle of everything. All of a sudden it was like everything went silent and these words just poured out on the paper. "<u>... to the heart that can't find faithfulness, to the body racked by sickness ... to the children with no father, ... to the widow who has lost her love, ... on the nights there's no one to hug ... so she stares into the darkness wishing he would call her name. But there's no one there to comfort her and her life is not the same ... there is an answer.</u>" The first verse speaks to the family. I don't take a lot of claim for that song, just as a vessel.

One day we had a format and I said "I feel we need to

take this in a little difference direction today ... I'm going to minister to widows today. I was the Executive Producer of the program by then, the head of the broadcast division, everybody that worked in television worked under me. I knew how to be the "boss," but I didn't know television, so I had called in all the key people that knew certain elements and made them supervisors over their areas. They were all very supportive as always. I started out the program with "today if you have lost your husband, please stay with us." I ministered that God is the husband to the widow. I didn't know if it made any sense, but then we did the song, "There is an Answer" and then we went on with the rest of the show.

In 1992, I was in California singing in a church in Walnut Creek. The pastor asked me to come back to his office before the service, and a lady walked in. She asked for a moment of my time. She was the pastor's secretary. Then she told me that her husband took very ill and she'd had to spend time every day with him at the hospital. He progressively got worse and worse, and the worse her husband, the more she felt separated from God like He didn't care about her situation. Her son would tape P.T.L. every day for her and she'd watch it when she got home at night. When her husband died, she felt such a loneliness for her husband. She felt like she was just another statistic. She wondered if God knew what she was going through. The peace she'd expected from God didn't come. Then she began feeling angry because God didn't understand her situation.

She came home, saw the tape sitting on the VCR and decided to watch it. And that's when we came on with the show I was telling about above. That days' program was the day her husband had died. She said, when I realized that God had gone from California to Charlotte N.C. and said this lady is going to need this tonight -- she said it was as if you knew me personally. But since you didn't know me personally, she said, I knew that God did. She said her whole life changed in that instant, all the despair, all the worry left her and she knew that God really cared about her.

The most wonderful part of being at P.T.L. was not the

television. It was just meeting people, connecting with people on Main Street, or receiving the letters. It didn't matter how I was being used for the Lord as long as I was being used. There were twenty-two hundred employees at one time, and the people for whom I worked were definitely not there for the money. I went to P.T.L. to serve God. I worked under the authority of the Lord.

I left the ministry in January of 1990, and it took me six weeks to recover. I was on the road for a while. Then I gave up the road work in order to be with my family more. I don't know what the future is. I have no aspirations to be anything more than what I am and whatever area God chooses to use me in, ... I work with television ministries helping them to find the best time to be on television to reach the audience they want to reach.

Ron Aldridge

Chapter 9

JOYFUL JEWELS

Miracle of Life

THE PEOPLE THAT LOVE HOME

The People That Love Home was started when Jeff Park and his wife started taking pregnant women into their home to keep them from having to have abortions. Many of the girls had been thrown out of their homes by their family or their boyfriends. When it got to be more than they could handle, a Girl's Home was built to provide a positive alternative to abortion for women in crisis pregnancies. Girls and women of all ages were accepted, as early as the second or third month of pregnancy until the baby was born. The home provided a healthy Christian family environment for the women and provided training and education while they were waiting for their babies to be born.

The Home gave a secure and stable environment for Christian growth and a support network for the girls. They had friends, fellowship, prayer-support, and counseling during the pregnancy to help them develop a positive and healthy attitude toward life. One of the main purposes was to nurture inner healing to the hurt surrounding the girl's pregnancy and the events leading up to it through prayer, study, and caring.

People That Love
HOME

The girls learned Christian responsibility and character development in order to prepare them for God's best in their lives. The staff encouraged the girls to continue their education by providing tutoring and guidance in academic matters. Each girl had a counselor assigned to help her in discerning God's will and direction for her life. Additional counseling was also available from P.T.L.'s professional counseling and pastoral staff.

Medical care was provided by licensed physicians and two licensed nurses who were on duty at the home to provide constant quality medical care. Childbirth classes were available as well as recreational and leisure time activities such as volleyball, swimming, paddle boats, concerts, hiking, camping, drama, crafts and handiwork. Homemaking skills were taught through assigned chores and participation in meal planning and preparation. Many opportunities were provided in devotion, Bible studies, worship services, and Christian fellowship. Each resident was also assigned a Christian Prayer Support Family who befriended, encouraged, and assisted her during her pregnancy. Counseling was also available for the whole family and the expectant father.

When P.T.L. closed and funds were no longer available, Jeff states, "we went back to the philosophy that we had before and started "Crisis Pregnancy Centers" which arrange housing, etc. for girls who are pregnant.

THE TENDER LOVING CARE ADOPTION AGENCY

"Before I formed thee in the belly, I knew thee; and before thou comest forth out of the womb, I sanctified thee." This is more than a beautiful statement by God. It is also the basis on which the Miracle of Life and Tender Loving Care Adoption Agency were founded. These P.T.L. ministries took a stand for the unborn children who were being murdered by abortion. They believed that man is created in the image of God, and they willingly fought any force that threatened to deliberately destroy God's creation. Many babies were saved through these battles and grew up to become happy children.

There were countless efforts by P.T.L. which stretched across America and served Christian families, expectant mothers, and their babies. Many of these are still continuing today as a result of their beginning at Heritage U.S.A.

WHAT IS TLC?

Tender Loving Care Adoption Agency is a non-denominational, non-profit Christian adoption agency licensed by the state of South Carolina. It is supported and sponsored by the PTL Home Missions and Heritage Village Church, and governed by a South Carolina Board of Directors.

More than just an adoption agency, TLC is actually a ministry designed to help expectant mothers determine the best plan for themselves and their children. Tender Loving Care Adoption Agency provides information, as well as emotional and spiritual support to residents of the People That Love Home as well as to expectant mothers in the local community and throughout the nation who request such service. Expectant fathers are also ministered to by the agency.

WHO DOES TLC SERVE?

Any expectant parent involved in a crisis pregnancy is invited to explore possible alternatives with Tender Loving Care Adoption Agency, and is under **no** obligation or fee for service. For more information, the expectant parent should write:

Leigh Ann Johnson
PTL Home Missions
Charlotte, NC 28279

or call: *(704)542-6000, ext. 2327*

Administrator Leigh Ann Johnson counsels expectant parents about adoption.

Along with its Christian ministry approach, the Tender Loving Care Adoption Agency is unique in the extent to which expectant mothers will be able to express their wishes and desires in the choice of adoptive parents.

Using both computer technology and personal and professional ministry, the Tender Loving Care Adoption Agency will select the best possible Christian home for each child served.

We recognize the fact that there are those Christian couples who are unable, for one reason or another, to have children and desire to adopt a baby. Tender Loving Care Adoption Agency desires to serve these families, as well as the expectant mother and her baby.

Tender Loving Care Adoption Agency is primarily involved in the placement of infants, however, we eventually hope to assist in the placement of older children, and special needs children.

WHO IS ELIGIBLE TO ADOPT?

The adoptive couple must be:
Committed Christians
Unable to have children naturally
Financially secure
Less than 40 years of age
and have a stable marriage

WHAT ARE THE ADOPTIVE COUPLE'S FINANCIAL RESPONSIBILITIES?

Non-refundable application fee $50
Home study fees (vary according to state)
Child placement fees
Medical and Hospital expenses for the expectant mother and her baby
Legal expenses

Eligible couples may fill out the attached "Request For Application" form.

114

Love Notes

Summer 1997   Jean Veckruise, Ph.D.- Director   SC - 803-548-6030

Joyful News from Christian Family Services & LifeHouse of the Carolinas

Letters, Beautiful Letters . . .
From a Birthmother to the Adoptive Parents of her child.
(Read why Birthmothers choose adoption.)

Dear Adoptive Parents,

Thank-you so much for the letter and pictures. It gives me so much comfort to know that David has a mother and father who love him as much as I do. I'm so afraid that he will think I gave him up because I didn't love him. That is so far from the truth. Children need so much in their lives, so much that I would never have been able to give him. I know he is so much better off with you.

When I received the first set of pictures of you and David, when you picked him up, I could see the love in your face when you looked at the baby and the love in your husband's face when he looked at both of you. I knew David was in the best home I could ever have picked for him. The only regret I have right now is that I didn't choose an open adoption. I think I would very much have liked to meet you and your family. It was so wonderful of you to think to trace his little hand. I will cherish it forever.

I want to thank you from the bottom of my heart for taking my little boy into your home and giving him all the things I couldn't. With you he has the family he couldn't have with me. He is so beautiful. He looks like my girls.

God bless you. I pray every night for you and I thank you for your prayers. Please be happy and know that you have a special place in my heart. Thank you again, With Love, Your Birthmother

From another Birthmother to CFS Office Staff:

My Dear Friends at Christian Family Services,

I truly want to just start by saying how much I truly love and appreciate you all for everything you've done for the girls and me. Our meeting has truly been a special blessing and you all have been special, kind, understanding and compassionate.

The decision I had to make was very hard, it's true, but out of all the bigger agencies, I know none of them would have given me the comfort and support like the people in the little office behind the cleaners (Smile, because bigger doesn't always mean better!) In me you all have a life-long friend, and I'm sure the feelings are mutual, so once again, I thank you all! Love Always,

From an Adoptive Mother to the CFS Staff:

To our Friends at CFS,

I feel terrible about not writing earlier to tell all of you how very much my husband and I appreciate everything you've done for us. I feel like we snatched up that precious little girl and whisked her away with hardly a thank you.

To say I've kissed Brittany's cheeks a million times is an understatement. My husband and I try to share her but I know I monopolize her time. I can't get enough of her.

Please accept our undying gratitude for all you've done for us. Gratefully,

Fall 1997 Jean Veckruise, Ph.D. - Director SC - 803-548-6030

Joyful News from Christian Family Services & LifeHouse of the Carolinas

God's Love Heals Broken Hearts Through Dawn, A Birthmother

It's always darkest before the dawn and this DAWN brought the sunshine of God's love into the lives of Lisa and Jim.

When Jim and I married in 1990 we had hopes for a future blessed with children. In 1994, God blessed us with a precious son, James Johanon. He was the light of our lives. We believed that God has completed us as a family. _On August 25th, our fourth anniversary,_ James turned blue in my arms and was rushed to the hospital. Weeks of testing uncovered that James had a severe genetic defect known as Severe Combined Immune Deficiency (SCIDs). The only cure was a successful bone marrow transplant. For the next two years we pursued a cure for James. Our fifth and sixth anniversaries were also marked by trips to the hospital. At one point I told Jim that I didn't think I could ever remember _August 25th_ with anything but sadness. Sadly, after a long and courageous fight, our beautiful son _died on October 16, 1996._ We were devastated.

Heartbroken, we found ourselves wondering if our shattered lives could ever be reconstructed. The effect of the experience was so great that we weren't even sure if we could count on God to help us recover our hopes and purpose for living. With time and Christian support we were able to begin again, but the depression and despair were still great. We realized that James would not return to us, but that we still needed and desired to be parents again.

We could get pregnant again but at the risk of having another affected child and enduring the suffering again. Or, we could adopt and possibly endure the rumored trials and tribulations of that route of parenting. Jim put it this way, "I do not have the emotional, spiritual, or physical reserves to endure another child suffering from SCIDs. I just remember that James needed help that no one on earth could give him. I felt that if there was some other child that needed help that I could give him, then I would do it."

After much deliberation we became convinced of God's purpose of adoption for the next child in our lives. But God called us especially to bi-racial adoption. And once we made ourselves obedient to His plan, God began to work. Less the 24 hours after we placed ourselves on the waiting list, we were called about a tiny baby boy who had been born two days earlier, three months premature. He was in the intensive care unit, healthy but weighing only 2 pounds, 6 ounces and uncertain prognosis. Our past history with hospitals was not a pleasant one, and we were tempted to question God's plan. But significantly we discovered that this tiny baby had been born on _July 15th_ and was _on a ventilator until Wednesday morning July 16th - exactly nine months to the day and date James came off of a ventilator the morning he died._ The fact that this baby had been born early was our sign from God that actually he was right on time for us. God was effecting our restoration.

As we flew through the processes and paperwork, God's hand was shown mightily. There were several families ahead of us - - none of which could be reached when this baby became available. Our homestudy was thoroughly completed in days when others had been waiting months. In the next few days our portfolio was

Winter 1997   SC - 803-548-6030

Jean Veckruise, Ph.D.- Director

Joyful News from Christian Family Services & LifeHouse of the Carolinas

DO YOU REMEMBER?

It's always fun to remember and we want YOU to remember with US as we count our ministry blessings.

Remember this story?

A young school girl, brutally raped by three men, didn't believe in abortion, birthed a beautiful baby who is now living happily with his adoptive parents.

And this one?

The Lord brought a name, Tracy, to a prospective adoptive mother's heart. She prayed every day for this woman, not knowing who this person was, but being obedient to God, she prayed. Five months later, a CFS staff member called her to tell her that five months ago, Tracy, a Birthmother, started working with CFS and chose their family to adopt her baby! Their family had been praying together every night for a Birthmother but never connected Tracy with being a Birthmother.

Why adoption?
Read these loving thoughts from a Birthmother to her Adoptive Parents.

"In your letter you mention that since you have adopted my baby you couldn't imagine life without her. I want you to know that I love my daughter with all of my heart and I knew when she was born I was going to have to give her up for adoption but they laid her on my stomach and I fell in love with her at first sight. She was so beautiful that it literally took my breath away. Her eyes were so big and round. She had fat cheeks, and she was my baby girl. I owed it to her as well as myself to at least try, but as time went on I knew that I couldn't give her what she needed. What I am trying to say is that the love I have for my baby girl is so great that I would not even think about disrupting the life that she will come to know with you and your family. So please don't even think about that. God bless you and your family."

These **beautiful stories happened** because **you prayed** and **you contributed** to our ministry.

If you *haven't supported* our ministry and would like to give to help save babies from abortion and be part of children's lives because you care about life, or for *those who once gave to our ministry but haven't sent a gift in awhile,* please take a look at your support giving and ask God if He would have you recommit to our work.

Please do consider our ministry in your year-end giving.

The following letter is from JoAnn Francisco:

Dear Reader,

We moved to South Carolina in January of 1984 when my husband took employment with the Security Department. I volunteered to help Lee Ann Johnson in the Girl's Home when it opened on July 4, 1984. We had ten girls to move in. One girl already had her baby and was staying with a shepherding family on the grounds. The purpose of the Shepherding family was to care for and nurture the newborn baby until they were actually placed in an adoptive home. The home not only helped the girls but it helped Christian couples who were unable to have children but very much wanted a child.

We had about a hundred calls a month from girls who were pregnant. We talked to the girls extensively on the phone and sent out applications. Out of those, about half would actually come in, and we only had room for 20 or 22 girls. The selection was done prayerfully, confident that the Lord would give us wisdom at the time we needed it. The response was so overwhelming, we couldn't handle it all, but we did set up a network of help across the country, other maternity homes, other counseling services. We never left a girl without an answer. We always gave her something to do, someone to call, somewhere to get help.

From the moment the girl walked in the door, we tried to minister to her. We worked at it with our whole heart. We prayed with her right away and let her know that this was a time of seeking the Lord, of finding out that God can be found. Our main message was that God could redeem the situations.

There were over 300 girls who lived in the home from the time it opened to the time it closed. There were close to 200 babies placed in Christian homes. There were many, many lives changed. Many of the girls were saved, and many rededicated their lives to the Lord. Many took on a clear and new understanding of what it was to walk with the Lord. The Home had a rippling effect. When the girls left, they went home to friends and families and touched those people. The baby touched people, whether he or she went home with the mother or went to an adoptive couple. The adoptive parents touched their world and the circle they came from. It was good to know how the Lord takes anything we have and all we have and makes it into something eternally good.

JoAnn Francisco

Chapter 10

MAGNIFICENT MINERS

Volunteer Ministry

The participants in the Volunteer Ministry at P.T.L. were another dedicated group. Many volunteers offered their time and talents each week throughout Heritage U.S.A. From the ministry's beginning, volunteers with a desire to work within a Christian ministry served as a vital part of P.T.L.'s outreach and growth.

Approximately 16 to 18 thousand volunteer hours were performed monthly by men and women working from two to forty hours each week in various areas of ministry from feeding the animals at Farmland U.S.A. to ushering during Sunday morning worship services at Heritage Church. One of the P.T.L. Volunteer Coordinators said, "Volunteers helped to fill gaps where the ministry can't always afford extra help. It was satisfying for them to know they were doing something not only for themselves but unto the Lord."

The volunteers offered a diversity of backgrounds and work experiences from retired executives to floral arrangers and included Heritage U.S.A. residents as well as those from surrounding communities. Even Heritage guests often volunteered during their stay whether it was for a few hours or several days.

The following letter is from Dorothy Bakker in Kentwood, Michigan:

Dear Reader:

I had written some children's stories which were recorded through a branch of the Singspiration Company. One was "The Jailer Who Was Freed." In 1986, I wrote the devotional guide for P.T.L. I also wrote some of the material for the large coffee table book about Jim and Tammy and P.T.L. I enjoyed working for P.T.L. because I knew the people were being helped. It was wonderful to see the whole project of Heritage U.S.A. unfold.

My main job through the years was with the producer's department as a writer. I wrote scripts for the interviewer so he would have direction for the interview and know what to ask.

One of the songs that used to be sung on P.T.L. said, "When you have nothing left but God - you have enough to start again" -- and I've often thought of this -- you can always start over and go on.

I have three adopted children, so I was very interested in the Girl's Home. I also love to go to yard sales. Many times, I found beautiful baby clothes that I could take to the girls. Once a girl came to me and said, "You don't know me, but before I gave my baby up for adoption, they let me pick out a little outfit for him. They said you had donated the clothes, so I was able to dress my baby boy before I gave him up. You'll never know what that meant to me."

I've just turned 62 and now I'm going to be freed up where I don't have to put in such long hours. I plan to live in Charlotte during the winter months and up at Lake Michigan during the summer. I plan to do some writing. I am excited and anticipating life!

Dorothy Bakker

The following letter is from Mary Davidson:

Dear Reader,

I had a very happy marriage, truly made in Heaven. My husband and I worked together, lived together and loved together. He died in June of 1978, and as long as I could go to the cemetery and take flowers every day, I was all right. But when winter came along, I began to go into a very deep depression.

In 1979, my sister came to live with me, I had a senile mother to take care of, and I couldn't seem to find a foothold. I went out and bought a super, deluxe stereo system and got some records I thought might cheer me up. But that didn't help. So I finally decided to take my life. I thought there was nothing for me to live for. My sister suggested that I turn on P.T.L.

I called into the P.T.L. prayer line to ask for help to overcome the depression. The depression persisted, so I decided to take sleeping pills that had been given to my husband. A call came to me from Pop Bakker asking how I was getting along and asking if they could do anything for me. That call saved my life. He invited me down to P.T.L. I went to visit in April. Jim met us and told us he was praying for me. I came back again to visit several times before my sister Francis and I decided to move to P.T.L. We bought a three-bedroom house so we could take in a student of evangelism. Our other sisters were taking care of our mother at that time. We moved in December 19, 1981 and were able to have Christmas with two other ladies, the Richardson sisters, who had moved from California to work the prayer lines.

They announced in Evangelism School that I had a room for a student of Evangelism, and a very lovely lady named JaNan Cline who was living in the campground with another girl named Bonnie Peters came to live with us. They were attending classes together and living in the smallest camper I've ever seen in my life in the campground. She came here and lived with us. Today she and her husband are traveling evangelists in Texas.

When my mother was ill, P.T.L. ran a special extension telephone line into my home, so I could be in touch with someone if I needed assistance. That was typical of the things that went on.

We would get calls from everywhere. I got one call from

a lady who was in a motel room with her teenage disabled child. She was going to kill her daughter and herself, and when she called and told me, we got the police from that town in that distant state to the motel where she was and stopped her from taking their lives. We had connections in any city in any state in the United States, so we could get whatever help was needed anywhere. While I had her on the phone, the supervisor was getting the police to the motel in that location.

Another lady called saying she felt so completely worthless that if she didn't find something worthwhile in her life, she was going to take her life. I told her, "Honey, God doesn't make junk. You just look in the mirror. You're a beautiful creation from God. You can't do that." At that time, I was working the Number One Phone. The number one phone rings almost constantly, because that's the one that rings first on the sequence line. As luck would have it, after she'd hung up, she called and got me back again. That was the only time I recall of anyone ever getting the same person back. She insisted on knowing who I was, so I told her, "There are four of us here called Mary, and I'm one of them." That was the only way I could give her a name. When she called back, she said, "Oh, I'm so glad I got you Mary. I want to talk more."

That was the whole heart of P.T.L., People that Love.

When Jim came home and the reporters gathered around him, with flashing bulbs, he called and asked if he could visit my sister Frances. I told him he could visit anytime he wanted to.

Now I'm busy in Bible study. Frances is working in what was the Original Heritage Church. She does courier type work. If not for the Heritage Village Church, the School of Evangelism, we would not have come here, I would have been lying on a hill top beside my husband.

Mary Davidson

The next letter is from Bob Panzion in Venice, Florida:

Dear Reader:
We lived just outside Detroit, Michigan, when we started watching P.T.L. on television. It was on two or three times a day. My wife would watch it in the afternoon and we'd watch it again at night. It was a good program all the way around, the music, the Bible teaching. We decided to visit P.T.L. in 1980 to see what it was all about. It was at that time that we went forward at the Barn and made a renewed profession of faith.

The day that we signed to have our home built, we came back on the grounds to stay at the hotel and saw all the television vans. That was the day that Jim resigned. We could hardly believe it. Julie and I worked as greeters out in front of the Grand several times a week meeting people from all over the country.

I worked as a volunteer on the telephones answering calls from people with a definite need. It was good to be able to talk to these people and help them in some way. I was also an usher and we helped with the Girl's Home for as many as eighteen girls at a time. We acted as a kind of parent for these girls who ranged in age from maybe 14 to around 20. Some of them had been kicked out of the houses by their parents. Others had been brought there by their parents. They were all professing Christian girls at that time. Some gave their babies up for adoption. Some kept their babies. We have heard from some of them since. One was from Michigan. She let her baby go, but she knew it was in a good home.

We started thinking about the fact that Jeff Park didn't have much help with the prison ministry. So I decided that I might be able to help him in some ways. We'd go up and give them writing materials and Bibles. About the third Wednesday, Jeff asked me to go over to the next cell block and witness to them. "No way," I told him. "I'm not here to witness. I'm here to push the cart for you." So that's what I did. I helped him out while he spoke to the guys.

The next day I went over and Jeff wasn't there yet. The

chaplain came down and asked for Jeff. He asked me to go up and get the cart ready while I waited for Jeff. So I did, and got everything arranged. Jeff still didn't show up. "Well, why don't you start your run?" the Chaplain asked. I ended up doing that whole jail. I didn't get out of there until 8:00 that night. I had to minister to them, do the very things I had said I would not do. There was one guy that called out to me, "Hey preacher..." And I told him, "I'm not a preacher. I'm a priest, because God made me that, but I'm not a preacher."

"I've got a problem," he said. "I'm in the last stages of AIDS."

"You've got to be kidding me," I said. We prayed together. He was moved to another part of the jail, and I found out later that the AIDS was in remission and the guy was getting better.

Bob Panzion

The next letter is from Zora Robinette in Ft. Mill, South Carolina. She was a very busy person, volunteering and working in one of the stores on Main Street. She was always interested in ministering to others.

Dear Reader:

I was working for the General Electric Company in Ft. Wayne, Indiana when I began watching the Jim and Tammy Show. In 1978, I came down and visited and fell in love with the place. Every chance I got, I'd bring a carload and come back and visit again. In 1982, I brought my youngest daughter down. She was 18, and she wanted to move here. She applied for work and they called in a couple of weeks and she came down and worked in the Little Horse. She lived in a tent by herself, through storms, but she had good neighbors that looked after her.

When G.E. started laying off, I felt such a drawing to come down here and when I was laid off, I decided to move. I sold my mobile home and moved here. I was so blessed to be here. My daughter and I got an apartment together. Some of the other family moved down later. I got a job in the General Store.

The love of God shed abroad was the greatest thing about this place. Everything was Christian oriented, everything oriented to praise God. Working in the store was a ministry. To be able to minister to the hurting people, to bless them in some way, even if it was just a smile, was a blessing. The staff would minister to each other. We'd go to the Upper Room and pray together.

I left in 1986 for eight years to go back up North. In 1994, the Lord led me to come back to Heritage. I came back to visit and felt like God was getting ready to do something here again.

The P.T.L. ministry dealt with hurting people more than some of the other ministries. Everything was oriented to feed the soul. No one could come here and not be blessed in some way. Everyone was touched by God in some way or another.

Zora Robinette

The next letter is from Vivian Jones in Ft. Mill, South Carolina:

Dear Reader,

I lived in Lawrenceville, Georgia, and moved to Charlotte in 1983 just before Thanksgiving. It seemed like there was something drawing me here. I didn't know anything about P.T.L., but a friend brought me here for a visit. When she came in, she said to me, "Vivian, something's telling me you're going to be living and working at P.T.L."

"Honey," I said, "that something is wrong."

I never dreamed of such -- never gave it a thought. But the Lord did open up the door and brought me here to Charlotte. After moving here, I came to P.T.L. and started volunteering on the prayer phones. At first there were five or six rows of men and women answering the phones. Calls came from everywhere from people needing help. We'd pray with them over their problems. I'd stay on the phones during the day and go to services at night. I'd be on the phones from 4:00 in the evening until midnight. I felt a calling that I was in the position where God wanted me to be on the phones, because of the experiences I'd had in my life.

There were a number of callers who were healed, but we didn't know who we were talking to and they didn't know whom they were talking to. Once a call came through, however, when I was on the phone and this person said, "I'm from Oklahoma, would you give me your name?"

"Vivian Jones," I said.

"I knew you," she said. "I recognized your voice on the phone, and I need prayer." I know that God directed that call to me -- and the other calls. I've had so many experiences through my life that God could use. When I was younger, I wanted to go to tell people about the Lord, but there seemed to be no way to do it until I began to minister on the phones.

When you're walking with the Lord and have the joy of the Lord, it overflows. Sometimes I have danced in the spirit and gotten up and run down the aisle and around the building. The devil would say to me, "You sure made a fool of yourself." That's the way the devil would try me, and I would have to rebuke him. I've had to battle Satan over and over again.

I am going to Alabama when I leave here, a place close to Auburn. I'll go to all the churches until I find the one where I'm supposed to be. My body can't take what it used to, I get tired and weak, but my spirit is the same. We must let the Holy Spirit have control of us.

Vivian Jones

The following letter is from Captain Danny White in Princeton, W.V.:

Dear Reader,

I wish to tell you about the ten most glorious years of my life. On November 28, 1981, I was shot in the back of the head. The doctor said I wouldn't live through the night. I was living in Ohio in 1984 when I came upon a program called P.T.L.

After watching several months, I decided to move to P.T.L. I volunteered at the auction and had the privilege of working with Bob Johnson and later serving God by working with Uncle Henry and Aunt Susan. I want to thank each and everyone at P.T.L. and New Heritage U.S.A. for your kindnesses. I love you all.

In Jesus Name,
Captain Danny White

The following is a personal letter from Dorothy Scott:

I Dorothy Scott (Dot) worked in the Guest Relations, Usher Deptment. I never considered my work as a job but as a ministry because all the Staff had the opportunity to pray and witness to the many hurting people that came to Heritage U.S.A. any time, anywhere on the grounds.

I had countless experiences with people that came there as a last resort in their lives. Many told me they were ready to commit suicide but someone told them to come to Heritage and there would be someone that would be happy to pray for them. They came and as a result went home feeling they had a new lease on life and praising God.

Numerous times people would tell me their marriages were on the verge of divorce, in other cases they had already divorced but came to Heritage and someone would counsel and pray with them or they would go to the marriage Workshops there, their marriages would be restored, they would go away happy and giving God the Glory.

Other times people would be sick in their bodies, soul and mind, someone took time to witness and pray for them and they went home changed, saved and healed in their bodies. While I was working there, my Grandson Matthew was born he only weighed 4 lbs. both of his kidneys were damaged, neither one of them functioned, but people at Heritage prayed for him and Thank God one kidney was totally healed, the other one was removed, his Doctors were amazed, they said all new cells were replaced in one. He had to stay in the hospital for about 2 months. He is 12 years old now and a healthy normal boy.

My personal testimony. I went in the hospital for surgery. I really don't know what happened but when I was put to sleep, the Doctors told my Family that I had a reaction to the drugs that I was put to sleep with and I would not live, in fact they thought I had already died, all my organs had stopped, I had no vital signs of life and had swollen so much I had no features at all. They also said if by a miracle I did live I would have brain damage and be like a vegetable the rest of my life, my Husband called Heritage from the Hospital to pray for me, they immediately started praying, early the next morning my Doctors came in my Intensive Care Unit room removed and disconnected all the monitors, oxygen, respirator, needles running from my entire body and told me I could go home that day. Well and with a sound mind. God heard the prayer. I give Him all the Praise, Honor and Glory, and will Thank Him the rest of my life.

I would have never believed there are so many hurting people in the world if I had not been there at Heritage U.S.A. and saw for myself how they came and went away blessed. I will always say the good there far out weighed the bad there. I praise God he gave me a chance to be a part of it.

                        Dot Scott

Dot Scott

The next letter is from Ann Spencer:

Dear Reader,
The first time we came to Heritage U.S.A. was to see if P.T.L. was real in September of 1980. We had watched a miracle working service where a child was healed. I was teaching handicapped children at that time as a volunteer in Pennsylvania, and when I saw this child it touched me so much that I called my husband and told him. The next day we watched the rerun and a few days later, he asked me if I'd like to come to P.T.L. My husband had never been to a church retreat much less travel 600 miles, but we came to P.T.L.
We were here three days and had a wonderful experience. I received the baptism of the Holy Spirit, was slain in the spirit for the first time, and was healed of rheumatoid arthritis. My left leg grew an inch. I had been wearing corrective shoes and didn't need them anymore. We were just taken up by the joy and love that the people shared and experienced while they were here.
No matter where you went on the grounds, you felt that love. We went back home not knowing what had happened to us. This was totally alien to our uprising. When we came back, God hit us with a prophecy. We went into camp meeting and Chuck Flynn was there. He called us out of the audience and prophesied over us. He told me that I taught handicapped children. That caught my attention. He didn't know me or what I did. A lady that worked here then came in and said, "I have a word for you from the Lord... you belong to the P.T.L. family... you're going to live here and work here."
We thought that was ridiculous. Our family didn't understand any that was happening to us. In February of 1981, the Lord said to my husband, "Go to P.T.L. and serve me, my son." My husband said he'd go, but I said, no way. In April we finally came down to camp meeting again. We walked around this place hand in hand, but our spirits were torn up because he wanted to come down and I didn't. On the way back home, I heard the audible words, "I will." My

husband had told God that he couldn't come if I wasn't going to be happy. When we got home, he went to bed, I went to the family room and buried my face in the floor and told the Lord every reason why I could not come here. Then he told me every reason why I needed to come. Finally I said, all right, Lord, but you'll have to prepare my heart.

We watched the Lord prepare my heart. Each morning the Lord would tell my husband that we should go to P.T.L. and serve Him. The next morning, he said to my husband, "Build a townhouse at P.T.L., my son." We ordered the very first home that was build at P.T.L. in June of 1981. Two years later, April of 1983, we moved. It was two years of training, learning to walk in His way. We dedicated our house to the Lord immediately.

My husband went to work as a maintenance man and eventually became Maintenance manager at P.T.L. I was his wife and homemaker, with no thoughts of serving or ministering in any way. Almost immediately, however, I was asked to be on the Prayer phones. That was a wonderful experience. I remember one young man from Tennessee who was paralyzed from a football injury. I led him to the Lord, and he was healed. But just talking to someone who was lonely was a blessing. I was on the phones for two years, then one day the Lord gave me a new ministry.

That was in March of 1985. In June, the Lord told me I was to serve in the Upper Room, but I was to do nothing. He would make the way. In July a lady in the Upper Room said the Lord had spoken to her and told her I was to be her assistant in the Upper Room. I started as a hostess in the Upper Room, assisting the pastors, greeting the guests as they came in. I worked there for four years, and I received as much as I gave.

People were so moved by the production at the amphitheater. They learned more than they'd ever known before about Easter. Many times they were people who'd never made a commitment to the Lord, never verbalized their commitment to the Lord. It wasn't that they didn't want Him, but that they didn't know what to do. Something like the Passion Play can bring a knowledge to you that you've never known. In January of 1989, I was asked to pastor in the Upper Room. I pastored as a volunteer every weekend or whenever the others were on vacation or in a meeting. I also taught seminars on Main Street until Heritage U.S.A. was shut down by Hurricane Hugo.

I've learned to wait on God. When God speaks it doesn't always mean do it right now. Sometimes there's a time of preparation. He tells you and then gives you time to adjust to the idea. God wants us to learn to rely on Him and your neighbor or friend who has God in him. We started sharing God's love with others through Bible studies. We can go to our friends and ask them to pray for us. The Bible says "Pray ye one for another." It doesn't say go to the big name, but "pray ye one for another that ye may be healed. Love your neighbor."

I feel I'm a diamond in the rough. I got a deeper walk with the Lord, a deep understanding of the Word and the value of the Word in our life, opportunities to share, and the healing of my body from my association with P.T.L. God brought me here as a rough diamond that he wanted to polish. In all his training, he has polished me, and now I'm going to go home and polish some more people.

Ann Spencer

Ruby Bee wrote the next letter:

Dear Reader,

I came to P.T.L. in 1986 purposely to do volunteer work after my husband died. I arrived on a Wednesday and went to work immediately on the prayer phones. The next Monday, I went to work at Fort Hope as well, starting with three days a week in the kitchen helping to serve the men their lunch.

Fort Hope was a home for men who had been on drugs and/or alcohol. Before coming to Fort Hope, they had to go through rehabilitation and be free of drugs. The directors of Fort Hope had Bible studies for the residents, a gym and a basketball court where they worked out daily. At one time there were 36 men there. All were assigned chores in the upkeep of the home, and nearly every one of them accepted the Lord as his savior while they were there.

I made a commitment when I came to Heritage U.S.A. to do whatever I could to work for the Lord. My way of doing that was to work on the prayer phones and in the kitchen at Fort Hope. Once during a telethon, I led 53 people to the Lord in three weeks, and there's no way to count the number of all the people led to the Lord just during the years that I helped to work the phones.

Even after P.T.L. closed, I continued to work with the prayer phones for the different organizations who came, and I still work for Co-mission, helping to get out their mailings. Co-mission came with Walk-through-the Bible when they came here, and they train people twice a year to go to Russia in teams of ten as missionaries for a year's period. These people come back changed. The Russian people are hungering for the Word of God, so many souls are saved. Up to this point, there have been more than 3,000 people sent over there.

I have quite a few senior citizens who work with me helping with mailings, making costumes for the drama, "Two Thieves and a Savior," and whatever else is needed. The women who help me all live here on the grounds and are so anxious to have a part of anything that might keep P.T.L. alive. I know this is because this place was dedicated to God.

You can still feel the atmosphere the minute you come in the gate. God resides on these properties. He's here regardless of what came in or who does what to whom. It is God's place, and we know that he still has a plan for it. It was a God-given idea.

Ruby Bee

Chapter **11**

FABULOUS FINDS

Other Ministries

The other ministries at P.T.L. included the Passion Play, the Campgrounds, the Playground, Petting Farm and Recreation area, the train and many, many more. No one could ever adequately portray the various goods that came from each and every one of these avenues. Even the children found diamonds in the rough — and are today ministering to others as a result of what happened at P.T.L.

The Amphitheater

THE PASSION PLAY

The Passion Play, entitled "The Ultimate Conflict," was designed to involve the audience in the dramatic events that surrounded Christ's final days on earth. From the tempting of Jesus by Satan in the wilderness to the agony of the crucifixion, the emotional impact was felt by every member of the audience personally and left memories that would never leave them.

While viewing the play, the audience laughed, cried, were angry, and filled with joy. The drama was produced in a massive stone wall which contained mountains, a pool, Herod's palace, an Upper Room, the Garden of Gethsemane, Jewish homes, and Christ's tomb. The director said that his purpose was "to show people their rightful place in Christ and that they don't have to be defeated because Jesus wasn't..."

The Passion Play was recognized as the most unique production of its kind. Thousands of lives were touched. People would go to see the play, sad and troubled and return, enthusiastic and joyful.

The Amphitheatre Where Passion Play Was Held

The following is a letter from Rebecca Martin and Yvonne "Birdie" Clark, owners of NarroWay Productions and producers of the new drama at the amphitheatre, The King's Arena. The theater has been brought back to life as they've followed God's guidance and allowed His Hand to work in their lives.

When contacted about their letter they stated, "We have tried to be brief yet still express the greatness of our God who never stops working for the good of those who love Him."

NarroWay
PRODUCTIONS

9700 Regent Parkway, Box 106   Fort Mill, SC   29715   (803) 802-2300   fax- (803) 802-2310

Dear Reader:

The year was 1986. Two women, serving as a music and drama team in a burgeoning Eastern Kentucky church, felt the calling of the Lord to form a corporation for the production of their Christian musical dramas. This "corporation" had existed unofficially in their hearts for years, even the name had already been given. But this year they were strangely impressed by the Lord, this corporation was to be more than a dream hidden in the heart. Although they hadn't the slightest idea what was to be the purpose or work of this new company, they contacted an attorney and followed his leadership in the procedure. NarroWay Productions, Inc. was born. And then it was to lie dormant for ten years.

The year was 1986. The media swarmed like maddened hornets on the grounds called Heritage USA. The world watched the crumbling of a religious empire. Some were thrilled at the revelation of such hypocrisy in the Church. Some felt betrayed by what seemed to be treason in the Kingdom of God. And the innocent who were caught in the sequence of events became punch lines for the world's big joke. It was not so much the descent of the place called Heritage USA as it was the fall of its Christian testimony that inflicted such pain. But it fell, and great was the fall of it. And then it was to lie fallow for ten years.

The year was 1996. Ten years later, the Lord brought together that sleeping corporation and the desolate place and God began to do, what only God can do. The "dry bones" of what once was the Heritage USA amphitheater began to clatter and dance and the Lord gave it a new name: The King's Arena.

Isn't God good? In the midst of destruction He was already in the process of restoration. The ending was really just a new beginning. It seems His greatest works are often rendered in silence. Never doubt, He is faithful.

To the innocent who were caught in the crossfire. To the generous who gave. To the warriors whose prayers did not cease. And to the devoted who never stopped believing that God is bigger than man's biggest mistake. Lift up your face to the heavens and praise Him, for He is faithful.

"This is what the Lord Almighty says: 'You say about this place, "It is a desolate waste, without men or animals." Yet in the towns of Judah and the streets of Jerusalem that are deserted, inhabited by neither men nor animals, there will be heard once more the sounds of joy and gladness, the voices of bride and bridegroom, and the voices of those who bring thank offerings to the house of the Lord, saying,

>   *"Give thanks to the Lord Almighty,*
>   *for the Lord is good;*
>   *his love endures forever."*

(NIV, Jeremiah 33:10, 11a)

Sincerely His,

K. Rebecca Martin and

Yvonne H. Clark

Left: K. Rebecca Martin, Right: Yvonne H. Clark

The next letter is from Harold and Marguerite Narber from Dover, Pennsylvania. They were members of P.T.L. from 1984 until it closed. They visited every year, attended workshops, seminars, The Upper Room, church services in the Barn, and some of the television broadcasting programs. They tell us that their lives were enriched as they sat under such men as C. M. Ward, Lester Sumralll, and Dan, Joe, and Sam Johnson.

Dear Reader,

P.T.L. was a place where denominational tags were left outside as you fellowshipped, prayed, and worshiped with people who loved Jesus and knew the joy of the Lord. The grounds were a safe place to walk after night or let children out to play without fear.

The Passion Play in the amphitheatre was a powerful presentation of the last week Jesus walked on this earth, his crucifixion, burial, and resurrection. It impacted the life of all who saw it.

In 1985, we took our children and grandchildren on vacation for a week. We went to the beach, other attractions, and spent three days at P.T.L. While there we all went to the Passion Play. Our grandson Bryan, who was five years old, watched intently, asking questions and believing he saw Jesus come out of the tomb and his ascension into Heaven.

Harold and Marguerite Narber

11/13/97

When I was a young boy my parents and grandparents took me on vacation to PTL. While we were there my family took me to see the Passion play. I don't remember everything about the trip, but I do remember the play and its message. "Jesus is alive". I was very excited to hear about Jesus and see what his life on earth was like and that he died on the cross for my sins.

About a year later, at the age of 6 I accepted Jesus into my heart as my savior. I am very thankful to have Godly parents and Grandparents that not only love me but have Jesus in their hearts also.

Bryan Stough

CAMPGROUNDS

The campgrounds were certainly different from campgrounds outside the Heritage U.S.A. area. There were different areas such as Praise Hollow and Holly Springs. The campgrounds covered about 350 acres of Heritage U.S.A. with two lakes included and a vast amount of wildlife. These were quality facilities for camping with 400 tent and trailer sites with water and electricity hookups.

The people who came to camp found instant friendships, because they were all Christians. They were friends already even though they hadn't met each other before. It was amazing to see how well people kept up their location. Lights were strung on awnings in front of trailers, and all the people in the park would visit, talk, and eat with one another. They would get together and walk to the workshops, seminars or meetings at night.

The following is a letter from Mr. and Mrs. Wayne McKee in Fort Mill, South Carolina:

Dear Reader,
We lived in Pennsylvania and came to P.T.L. first on vacation in 1979, stayed in one of the lodges with some friends and fell in love with the place. It was like we were in another world. When we first came we were transferred by bus down to Charlotte for seminars and meals. Every year after that, we came on vacation and went through the Wagon Wheel.

When my husband retired in 1983 or 84, we wrote to P.T.L. and found out about parking a camper during the winter months. They had an opening for a winter campground host and asked if we would be interested. Of course, we felt that was God opening a door for us. We met all the campers as they came in and took care of the campgrounds. We helped them set up and turn on the water and electricity. We were in Sugar Creek Campground first. After about a year and a half, my husband had bypass surgery, and we were moved from Sugar Creek to the smallest campground so I could take care of it by myself. When my husband got better, we were moved to Breeze Hollow Campground.

We would walk through the campgrounds several times a day checking on things and visiting with the people. We still hear from many of those campers who still remembered the wonderful times at P.T.L. Everybody from the campground went down to Camp Meeting every night. One of the campers took me to the hospital to pick up my husband and bring him home. The campers were a happy lot, very few were ever disgruntled in any way.

When the campground closed, my husband and I volunteered in the Love Center for a while and then volunteered with Jeff Park in the prison ministry. I'm the secretary for the Prison ministry now. Jeff believes in what he's doing and is the hardest worker I've ever known.

Mr. and Mrs. Wayne McKee

HERITAGE VILLAGE CHURCH AND MISSIONARY FELLOWSHIP

The Children's Ministries of Heritage Village Church sponsored exciting activities for the children on the grounds in addition to the Waterpark, playgrounds, train, and other fun things to do. On Fridays, they had Kidcinema (free cartoons and movies in the Chapel By the Lake). Kidskate was on Saturdays in the Recreation Village Family Center, and Kid fun acivity time was Saturday afternoon with cartoons, puppets, games, refreshments and other "kidevents." A Sunday morning children's service was always held where the youngsters could worship the Lord and learn about His Word. Lessons from the Bible came alive with puppets, clowns, music, stories, games and video presentations. After the worship service, the young folks were transported to the HVC Total Learning Center for Sunday School classes.

Children, ages 5 - 12, also had the opportunity to attend Day Camp, with Bible adventures, nature studies, field trips, water sports, games, hiking, crafts, tournaments, skating, antique car and train rides. Heritage Village Church also offered child care for parents visiting and working at P.T.L. This

Front of the Grand Hotel

was a total learning center which provided the highest quality child care.

The ministry of Heritage Village Church and Missionary Fellowship was one of love, reaching out to the body of Christ, developing mature Christians, and spreading the Gospel around the world. The Heritage Grand Ministry Center served the ministry as a worship center and retreat facility for the Body of Christ. It was not a public facility, but a Christian retreat center, building up the Body of Christ around the world.

FARMLAND U.S.A.

Nestled at the end of the road leading by Kevin's House, away from the bustle of P.T.L.'s major activities was farmland U.S.A. where young and old alike could enjoy a unique glimpse into farm life of yesteryear. At Heritage Farm, located within Farmland's tranquil setting of trees and gentle sloping hills, one could find the sights and sounds of farming days in the 19th Century. Among the farm's displays was the Heritage Petting Zoo featuring a variety of furry animals from camels to miniature goats, all ready to greet visitors. Trail rides were also offered with guides and providing a scenic tour through the wooded and streamlined area. Pony rides were also available and various farm displays, depicting rural life during the Victorian era, including a large red livery stable complete with a hayloft, an outdoor bake oven, a corn crib, a working windmill, a smokehouse, and a dry seed house. A four-bedroom Victorian farmhouse overlooked Lake Carolyn. It had a white-railed front porch.

HERITAGE USA ACCOMMODATIONS.

The Heritage Grand stood majestically on the shores of Lake Heritage with more than 500 rooms offering the ultimate in accommodations at a Christian Retreat. Each room had the finest in bedding and furnishings. To the south, the Heritage Inn offered 96 units for overnight occupancy. Five Heritage Inn rooms and 24 at the Grand were designed for the handicapped.

A Camel Ride

E.J. Scofield & Billy Scofield

Thousands of P.T.L. partners and their families spent many hours of enjoyable leisure and relaxation in the majestic Heritage Grand Ministry Center. Tobacco, drugs and alcohol were not allowed in the Ministry Center or anywhere on the grounds. No running was allowed, proper and modest swim wear was required.

The Presidential Lounge was available for the P.T.L. President Club Members and Lifetime Partners on the third floor of the Heritage Grand Ministry Center. It was tastefully decorated in a Victorian motif and offered an opportunity to relax, read, write home, watch The P.T.L. Club on television, and fellowship with others. It was a perfect place for quiet meditation. Soft music, friendly hostesses and fresh hot coffee provided a refreshing atmosphere for partners yearning to "get away from it all."

The Family Center offered intellectual games like chess and checkers or those of dexterity and skill like table tennis, pocket billiards and select video games. It also provided the Roller Skating Rink. Recreation Village had a ten-hole Miniature Golf Course and eight lighted tennis courts. Bicycles could be rented and the antique car rides and carousel were there too. The Lake Heritage Boat House offered terrific on-the-water fun with rented paddle boats. An Olympic-sized swimming pool was available at the Recreation Village. The Heritage Children's Railroad provided further pleasure and excitement as it carried passengers around Lake Heritage and Buffalo Park. Buffalo Park had picnic tables, hibachi grills, big shade trees, playground equipment, and musical shows. It was one of the most popular Heritage U.S.A. gathering places. There were Old West Buildings and a stagecoach, slides, and swings. The Buffalo Park Lakeside Theater offered outstanding musical and variety programs for the entire family. The Heritage U.S.A. Talent Show allowed those from six to 96 to display their abilities on the Lakeside Theater stage. The Heritage Grand Christian Dinner Theater offered pleasant evenings featuring Bob & Jeanne Johnson, the P.T.L Singers and Orchestra, Derek Floyd, and the Celebration Singers. An elegant dinner was served before each evening performance.

*Dick Alexander — Presidential Lounge
and Mary Lou Edwards*

The Train

Hank Scofield & Children, Jenesa & Jared at Water Park

Chapter 12

PRICELESS PROMISES

Workshops, Seminars, Musicians

The workshops, seminars and the numerous musicians were some of the richest sources of diamonds and hidden treasures offered at P.T.L. Workshops helped to repair, heal and restore lives. Couples whose marriages were in trouble came there to talk with counselors. Up to ninety people came a day, close to 10,000 couples, and 8,000 marriages were restored.

Thousands of individuals and couples annually had their lives changed through the workshops and the workshop exercises which employed Biblical principles in ridding individuals of past and present mental and emotional hurts. Marriage I Workshops were held on a monthly basis and Marriage II sessions were presented at various times. Many individuals also had their lives transformed through the Inner Healing Workshops.

The seminars were so valuable. Lives were transformed through the Bible Seminars led by gifted teachers such as Evelyn Carter Spencer, Phillip Powell, Richard Weylman, Paul Tinlin, David Lewis and C. M. Ward. These seminars were held twice daily, Monday through Saturday. Some had problems so deeply ingrained in their subconscious that they despaired of any hope every coming their way, but the counselors and teachers were well trained in the things that were needed. They knew exactly how to guide each group. Other specialized seminars were held such as Financial Seminars which taught how to stay away from financial difficulty, estate planning, and good stewardship. These people who went through these workshops and seminars went back home with changed lives to counsel others with the same problems ... at church, home, in their neighborhoods and cities. Because they had been helped, they wanted to help others.

The musicians were another source of diamonds wherever they were playing, in the lobby, on Main Street, in Camp Meetings, Sunday Services, anywhere and everywhere, they blessed everyone with whom they came in contact.

The Celebration Singers — Who Came Twice a Day to Sing in the Presidential Lounge During the Holiday.

Bob and Jeanne Johnson

This letter is from Joy Towe:

Dear Reader,

I was drawn to Heritage U.S.A. because I had been watching the P.T.L. program for quite some time. One morning I was watching when an anointing came about, and I said, "Oh, God. That's what I'm longing for ... for something to be real." I decided to visit the grounds in 1985. I was impressed and decided I wanted to settle there where there were so many Christians around. I needed the friendship and the environment.

When I moved, I was an evangelist and musician and traveled quite a lot. I thought I would make Heritage my headquarters and still go out and share in praise and worship. But it wasn't long until my traveling ceased. Musicians were much in demand on the grounds and I became one of the staff members that played in various areas. My chief post was in the lobby of the hotel. I called that my pulpit. I played music that would glorify the Lord and spread His presence. More than once, someone came up and told me, "While you were playing, this person received healing." People would come in looking lonely, depressed, grasping for something. They would leave with a gleam on their face, because someone had reached out and paid them some attention.

Sometimes I would play a song and someone would come up and ask, "How did you know that was just what I needed to hear?' I was there in the lobby when they came back from the Upper Room or from the Passion Play. I was in the hub where I could watch the people mingle. I was also blessed to be able to bring the devotions several times a month in the Presidential Lounge. I also played in the cafeteria where there were two lines going constantly. I was also the organist at the camp meeting and blessed to be able to minister there.

Joy Towe

Joy Towe

Having Fun at Heritage!

A TYPICAL DAILY AGENDA

A typical daily Agenda for Heritage U.S.A. might include ongoing anointing services in the Upper Room, Intercessory prayer sessions in the Upper Room, Child Care program in Total Learning Center, and a Bible Seminar in the Lower Chapel. A Ministers & Spouses Seminar might be in the Heritage Grand Ministry Center, and Devotions for President's Club Members were held in the Presidential Lounge. Live productions of the P.T.L. Club were in the Studio, while a "Biblical Principles of Financial Freedom" seminar might be held in the Heritage Grand Ministry Center. An "Estate Planning" seminar would be on the second floor of the Grand Palace Cafeteria, Baptism services in Heritage Grand Pool, and Praise Services in the Upper Room. A "Lookin' Good" seminar might take place in the Grand Palace Cafeteria, and Family night services were held at Heritage Village Church, Camp Meetings in the Ministry Broadcast Center, New Hope Fellowship for alcoholics and their families in the Total Learning Center, and the Passion Play in the Jerusalem Amphitheater.

If it was a weekend, there would also be the weekly auction, Children's Church, Sunday School, and Heritage Village Church Services, morning and evening.

For food, recreation, and shopping there were always Tony's Sidewalk Cafe, Bentley's, Grand Palace Cafeteria, Heritage Court, McMooses's Granny's Kitchen, Little Horse, Susie's Ice Cream Parlor, the Recreation Village Family Center, Heritage Children's Railroad and Golden Carousel, Lake Heritage paddle boats, bicycle rentals, antique cars, miniature golf, horseshoes, shuffleboard, tennis, the waterpark, the Village Pool, the General Store, Noah's Toy shoppe, Jerusalem Shoppe, Heritage Gift Shoppe, Goodie Barn, Tours, and Billy Graham's Boyhood Home among others.

The Water Park

Water Slide

The Barn Where Meetings Were Held

Chapter **13**

RARE RICHES

Residents, Visitors, and Special Friends

The following letters and contributions give us a small taste of the inspiring and wonderful residents of Heritage, and visitors and special friends of P.T.L. These people and their stories are sparkling diamonds resulting from their relationship with or their coming to P.T.L. They took away with them hidden treasures which are shining in their lives today.

Stores on Main Street

It is only fitting that two of Myra Bumgardner's poems begin this chapter. Her shop called Cherubs Landing was one of the most attractive on Main Street, and her poetic words are some of the most beautiful and thought provoking that you will find. Today Myra uses the artistic talents God has given her in writing and painting to reach out to others for Him. I believe you will be inspired, as you read her poems and the accompanying letter, to start your own search for hidden treasures.

When We See As We Are Seen

Tho' loved ones have gone from this world
To a world mine eyes cannot see,
Still e'er they live in joy and praise
Somewhere beyond the sea.

The grief I bear is for myself alone,
For they are well and free.
No tear-stained robes do they wear
Somewhere beyond the sea.

They stand bright-shining as the sun,
And they walk on streets of gold.
They talk with Abraham, Isaac, and Jacob,
And they never shall grow old.

And when we see as we are seen—
Each mystery is at last unfurled:
The joy we'll share with loved ones there
Has no equal in our visible world.

—Myra Eaves Bumgardner

Let Us Love One Another

Of one mind, with one accord—
In unity, they awaited the Promise.
Those pioneer soldiers of the early church:
Each loving the other – even doubting Thomas.

We speak of the world: of its lack of love,
Of its deception and its selfish ways.
"The noble gesture is dead," we say.
"It's not like in the good ol' days!"

But what of the church: the exemplary light?
Are we united in love as of old?
Will the world believe the Messiah has come
When it sees us uncaring, fragmented, and cold?

How our Lord must grieve, and even weep
As we crucify one another:
As we back-bite and devour—
Not caring, nor preferring each other.

"My church must love as I have loved,"
Whispers the Shepherd to my soul.
"Each esteeming other better than themselves,
For it takes each part to make the whole."

My heart senses despair in His cry.
As if our Lord doth travail in pain.
Could we, Christ's church, be guilty
Of crucifying Him again?

O church! Let us walk as He has walked!
Let us LOVE one another!
Let us extend one hand to the lost—
The other hand to our brother.

For when that trump shall sound,
And the dead shall arise;
Of one mind, with one accord—
In unity we shall ascend the skies!

—Myra Eaves Bumgardner

Dear Reader,

For the first three years after being saved, I thought God had something more spiritual for me to do than paint. We held Bible study in our home every Tuesday night. There was a precious girl in my class once who told me, "If God gives you a gift and you don't use it, it's like saying you don't appreciate it and throwing it in the wastepaper basket. And God will take it away from you. So I got my easel out that afternoon and set about painting illustrations for Bible verses. I also started writing poetry and found out that the poetry and paintings went together. Now the prints are all over the United States and abroad. I know that every step I took up until the moment that I knelt by that easel was preparation for what God was preparing me to do. Now He seems to be leading me more into the writing.

I lost my husband suddenly to a stroke when he was 58. During that time, God gave me such a wonderful faith and strength. That's when God started breaking me and removing all the props. Since that time, he has taught me that I can do things I never thought I could do.

Since my husband has died, God has taken me into the pitfalls of being single, the vulnerability, he has shown me that I'm human just like everyone else. He has introduced me to myself and my flesh, which I have not liked, but it's been a wonderful experience too. He has taught me to never give up, out of the fragmented brokenness of our lives, God is creating us all. Until we look at our own humanity, our own flesh, how can we look at the lost and say God is your redeemer.

I believe he is exposing us to our humanity so he can equip us to go outside the four walls of spiritual superiority and touch the hurt and needy and lost.

Myra Bumgardner

Darryl Bunch is a very interesting individual with an unusual story. In spite of the many problems he has experienced in his life, Darryl has given unselfishly of himself and his security business when needed. He and his lovely wife, Mary Jane, know from personal experience the treasures that are to be found on the grounds of Heritage USA. They are still available with their security services today to make sure that the residents feel safe and protected when on the grounds. Darryl is working on a book entitled, *"Mixed Blessings in the Storm"* about his experiences. For more information, write Darryl Bunch, P.O. Box 11348, Charlotte, NC 28220.

Dear Reader,
I ran a security and investigation company in Ohio. A divorce and the worst time in my life in 1987 brought me here. What Jim had gone through with the publicity and the scorn from the media actually gave me strength to go on during this very difficult time in my own life.

I was trying to keep ahead of my own problems. I was wrongfully accused of a crime, and in the next short while, lost my wife, my family, my home, my business, and my reputation. I thought my life was over. I finally reached what I thought was the low point of my life, and left town and came to Fort Mill and took a job with the National Security Firm. What happened thereafter has been amazing. God has given me a new business, a new home, a new wife and family.

Seeing Jim go thorough his problem made me see that I could go through what I had to face back in Ohio. A man like that - I saw God in him, I'm sure he had done wrong. He was a man after all, and sometimes a man loses sight of where he should be going, but seeing him gave me the strength to go on. If God could do that for him in this huge scandal, he would help me.

After the divorce, I no longer had a business or a job, but I had my two teenage sons with me. When I came here, a man who knew my father called and gave me a job in charge of a retirement home. It was just what I was looking for -- not a lot of pressure, and that's where I met Mary Jane my current wife.

I was later hired to do security for the 21-day telethon, so I provided all the security, traffic direction, parking lot, at costs. I was not even looking for a pat on the back. I just wanted to see this place restored. For the past year, I have provided free nighttime security, because God has put it in my heart to do that. I learned a long time ago not to question Him.

Darryl Bunch

Caleb Caywood is a very sincere person who has found true happiness through his service to God. Today he and his wife are called "the Joyful Caywoods" in friendship circles, because of the way they are constantly helping others in need.

Dear Reader,

I had been married 24 years when my wife led me to the Lord on Halloween of 1971 after having been an atheist all those years. We had four children, but to my dismay, we ended up divorcing. I did not want a divorce. I still wanted her back, so I was miserable. Sometime during that time, God told me that someday I would have a wife who would love me a hundred times more than the wife I was losing, but it was hard for me to believe at the time.

A friend of mine who had bought a partnership down here invited me to visit. He paid my way from Texas, bought me a membership and encouraged me to come down here and start a new life.

I found it was good to make a clean break. Our children were pretty much grown. So P.T.L. was like a haven for me, a safe port. I loved it here. It was so fabulous. We moved down August of 1987. P.T.L. was like heaven on earth. We had dinner theaters at night, and there was always so much going on Main Street. I volunteered on the prayer phones. It was a real blessing. I got more out it than the people. One day, a woman called me and said she was going to kill herself because her husband had died a year ago that day. I found out that she was from Oklahoma and began talking to her. I was able to keep her from killing herself that day. We had calls from Satanists who were nasty, but the Lord gave me a beautiful way to get them off the line. I'd say, "God loves you. Jesus loves you. I just pray that Jesus is going to come in your life and turn your life around and that you are going to work for him instead of Satan." As soon as they started hearing that, they would hang up.

Once a girl called in who needed $239.11 or her electricity was going to be cut off. I told her how God loved her and that he was able to do more than she could hope or pray for. I prayed that God would give her the money in a way that she would know it was from Him. The next day, she called back, and the call came to my phone. She had gone to her mailbox and in the mail was a check for that exact amount of money from someone she'd lent it to twenty years before. God knew who to put the calls through to.

I decided since I was single to apply to go to Siberia or Russia with Campus Crusade. I had all these papers to fill out and was sitting there at McDonalds, praying and looking at the papers. "Lord," I said, "you know I am lonely . . . " And it felt as though He told me, "You will meet your wife at Campus Crusade Training in two months ... fill out the forms." So I filled out the forms, went for staff training, looking behind every bush and palm tree to find her. I met Ellen when I went by to meet with one of the men who were supposed to advise me on raising support. She told me her husband of 51 years had died and how for 40 years she had witnessed to him. She said he was saved before he died. We hit it off right away and were later married.

Caleb Caywood

The Lake

Time Share Around the Lake

Because of the treasures that Marty Heath found at P.T.L., she is a wonderful neighbor and servant of God. Always "doing for others," Marty is an inspiring example of the brilliant diamonds still quietly serving God on the grounds of Heritage today. A very outgoing person, an inner joy radiates from her smile.

Dear Reader,
My husband John Heath passed away two years ago. We were living in Tampa, Florida. He had just retired as a Lt. Col. From the Air Force, and I was working in a church in Odessa Fl with Marion Lamb who was a retired psychotherapist. At the church they had a P.T.L. food and clothing closet. This was designed by Jim Bakker as a People That Love Center. They would send us boxes and boxes of Bibles, tracts, and literature. I was working in that center and got acquainted with all of this and had watched P.T.L. on television.

I had a call from my son in Charleston SC about that time asking that I come up because their baby was ill and they were both working. My husband was working at the Tampa Housing Authority, so I said yes. I drove up and was with them for a week and the baby was still sick. So on the weekend while they were home, I turned on the television. Jim and Tammy were talking about Heritage U.S.A. and Fort Mill, S.C. I checked the map and found out it wasn't that far. I left on Saturday and arrived about 4:30 in the afternoon. I found my way down to the log cabin welcome center. I asked if I could get a room for the night. She said we have a women's conference on and there's no room available. "You know," I said, "I really feel like the Lord has led me here, and if he led me here, he'll have a room for me. So if you don't mind, I'll sit in your fireplace room here and you can call me when one is available."

So I went in and had hardly sat down when they called my name. A woman over in one of the places on the lake had taken ill and had to leave very suddenly. "If you want that room," she said, "it's available and it's been paid for." So of course, I thanked her and went over. I had the whole loft to myself. The next morning when I got up it was like Jesus took me by the hand and he said, "Come I want to show you everything that is here." He took me everywhere. He told me he had called Jim and Tammy to be head of the place. He took me down to the barn to the Sunday morning service. After that he introduced me to Jeff Parks and told me had quite a ministry here and perhaps I'd like to join Jeff in soul winning. I told him I'd like that. Then he took me to the Upper Room. That is when I heard about the many people who had received miraculous healings in the Upper Room and perhaps I would like to write down the names of any family or friends who had salvation or healing and drop them in the big prayer bin.

Jesus said, "Come," and he took me to the hotel. "Isn't it grand here?" he said. Everyone was so happy. "Look at the people's faces," he said. "Everyone is so happy here. My children come from all over the world because the presence of the Lord is here. One day you'll get acquainted with a lot of them." He took me on one of the trams and around to the campgrounds. We had a motor home. Jesus said, "Perhaps you'd like to come up and stay in the campground." He took me here. He led me there. He introduced me to different people, and joy just filled my soul. And I knew at that time, I was coming back.

And sure enough, a few years later through a series of miracles when there were thousands on the waiting lists to get homes down here, he led me to Nancy Bowman. She told me about the waiting list, but she knew of a party on Sweet Gum who was thinking about selling their house. We did and they needed a big down payment on the house so they could build their home, and they also wanted us to rent the house back to them for seven months. So we gave them the big down payment and allowed them to rent the house for eight months. And within eight months, we were here.

Our big retirement house had been a dream for years, two real estate agents, one from the church and one, a Jewish man who lived on the street. I told them we needed to sell the house in two weeks. They couldn't believe I was asking that, but they decided they'd like to work on it. This was on a Thursday. We all prayed together and asked the Lord to sell the house within two weeks because he had made available to us a house up here. When we finished, the Jewish real estate said, "Why don't you let me run an ad in Sunday's newspaper and have an open house on Sunday?"

We left for the weekend, and when we got back he told us two men had come to the house, looked it over, loved it, and said, "we'll buy it." "Your house sold in two days!"

The Lord had healed me of osteoarthritis in my back and arms and an edema where my legs swelled up. There was no cure for either of them, but he showed me that up here I would become involved in the healing of others.

I stayed at Heritage because of the people. We bought a cottage in Hendersonville where we go to in the summer. In the winter time, we'd go to Florida and camp. We'd stay at Heritage in the spring and the fall. Jack died two years ago. I'm finding out now that my life is closing down. I love people and I like doing things, the symphony and the theater.

Marty Heath

Marty Heath

Helen Albright and her husband Bob have been through tremendous trials, but they have come out of them with a faith that still shines brightly today.

I think the marvelous lesson that Bob and I have been learning these past months is that our Lord's magnificent miracle of healing is spiritual as well as physical. He has always had His loving Hand on us, but we didn't always recognize this, and Him, in everything.

Let's take Tuesday, Sept. 20th - - Bob was surely led to take me to our doctor instead of keeping a very long-standing appointment with our lawyer. And here I'll say, "Praise God." Our general doctor disappeared for a minute; then came back to say, "I have just admitted Helen to Charlotte Memorial, and they want to know, 'Are you coming in before lunch, or after lunch?'" Surely our God had intervened again, and just in time. I didn't get home for six weeks. And then He brought our dear son and his wife to Charlotte to be with Bob and me.

And then on Sunday night before Monday's surgery Pastor Jeff Park and Dee showed up in my hospital room - like old home week - What a joy! And then, after two Sunday services and "Sunday Night Live", Pastor Sam and Joyce came - It must have been 10 o'clock - I was so surprised and delighted. God must have let them know how much it meant to me.

So now, Monday and surgery. Actually, the next 10 days are a blank to me, in a coma. But Praise God, He was right there. Apparently, the 4-way by-pass went very well and Bob and the children heard the good news. I say, "apparently" because some hours later a complication was discovered. But of course, God knew what was needed, and the surgeon had to perform the second operation that same day.

And this is where the miracle continued, because I did not wake up when I should have. The general consensus of the hospital staff was that I had had a massive stroke and was brain dead. They took Bob aside to a conference room and told him that. How dreadful for him!

But our God, and prayers, and Bob, and the surgeon would not let me go. Ten days later, in God's loving mercy, and perfect wisdom, and sovereign power, my Heavenly Father woke me up. Bob's face was just inches away when I opened my eyes. And he asked, "Is there anybody in there?" And I said, "Yes, I'm in here." Praise God, praise God, Praise God! And with no damage at all. And of course, the Lord upheld me all through a prolonged recovery, and I really needed Him.

May I take a few more minutes to thank some people. First of all, Pastor Sam Johnson, and every one of you, for your caring and your prayers. There are no words! And Pastor Bob Dearborn - Every day for six weeks, he came, and his prayers helped sustain me. (In truth, the hospital staff thaought he was a little crazy!) And there were the beautiful flowers from our beloved "choir rejects" - the ushers. And after I got home, Debbie Fender had organized the "Women's Outreach" to bring in our dinners. And, the many, many cards and calls.

What a privilege it is to belong to this Christ-centered fellowship. We want to thank you all for being a marvelous witness to our children, as the Lord again demonstrates that "All things work together for good to them that love God."

1988

Helen P. Albright
R T Albright

Paige Orange and his wife have been "heirs" of the wonderful treasures to be found through P.T.L. programs and people since 1983. They give God the credit for bringing them to P.T.L. and for all the marvelous events that occurred. People like the Orange family have blessed me in being able to be with them and listen to their story.

My new friend, Ray Walters,   May 28, 1997

At long last! Through this book God will get the credit and praise for what really happened at Heritage USA.

I am the blessed heir of the events that follow and it is my delight to make you a joint-heir.

My first trip to PTL was late '83 or early '84. The only buildings that I recall was what is now the Time Share offices (Defender Resorts), the Chapel-By-The-Lake, The Wagon Wheel Restaurant, The Upper Room and the TV studio. I spent my days on company business and my wife, Joanne spent her days on the grounds of PTL. At her urging, I came at night for the TV program taping. A dear, sweet black lady greeted us at the entrance to the TV studio (you could not enter without first being hugged). We were first to arrive. As the lines began to lengthen, she asked if we would mind letting a gentleman go ahead of us. He was barely mobile on elbow crutches kind of half shuffling, half dragging his feet. As we waited, he very casually said that "three months ago, I was dead." That got my attention. He told of how he had reacted to an injection (dye, I think), had died, and what he experienced while dead. Today it is referred to as a 'near death' experience despite the fact the person involved has no doubt that he actually died. (I've known several such people). He told of being in Heaven, its indescribable beauty, seeing family and friends, of seeing the Lord. He also had no desire to return but was told he must. As he reenter-ed his body and began to stir, his wife was advised he would never be anything but a vegetable. But here he was three months later talking to us. With a boldness I had never seen before, he said "I've come to be healed and I'm not leaving until I'm healed." He was with a bus group from Pittsburgh and some benefactors had made it possible for he and his wife to come. The doors opened and we went in for the taping of the TV program. The next night my wife and I were riding the tram, passing the waterwheel and she said, "isn't that your friend from last night?" Sure enough, there he was literally skipping across the parking lot. We didn't see him again but the next day about 11:30 we were leaving a motel in Camden, SC and my wife said look what's on TV. It was PTL and there was a big, burly, black man being interviewed by Jim & Tammy telling about how he had been a part of a healing service in the Upper Room the night before. Though we didn't hear them say so, we somehow knew the person being talked about was the man from Pittsburgh. The following day we were in a Jacksonville, Fl. home and were leaving with our hosts for lunch. I went to turn off the TV and there on the screen was the man from Pittsburgh, in his familiar western type blue jacket and cowboy hat. He verified the roll of the black man as he told the story of his healing. How blessed we were to have talked with him and then as we travelled south to hear on different days the completion of the story.
It was also on this first trip that my wife discovered she had left her nitroglycerine at home. She prayed that she not need it while at PTL. She never needed it again. Healed? She says so!
****
On one of our visits to PTL, my wife and I were waiting in line at the Morrison's Cafeteria, at the opposite end of the mall from the Heritage Grand Hotel. A couple ahead of us were talking and he said "I can hear everything she says." My wife, having defended her southern accent many times while living in Buffalo, NY, thought he was just one more making comment on her accent. As we talked with them we found his hearing had been restored in the Upper Room and with his hearing aid now in his pocket, he was enjoying hearing without it. (Their last

known address: Charles M. Quick and Dorothy Bressler, Before 124 Whistle Stop Rd, Baltimore Md., 21220).

****

On another visit my wife and I were in the Upper Room where Uncle Henry and Aunt Susan were ministering and a man stood up and told this story: 'An airline pilot, he had a few hours between flights and came to the Upper Room. He told about his brother, alone in a motel room in Georgia, had decided to end his life. He went to turn up the volume on the TV to drown out the noise of the gun he was going to use. At that moment, Jim Bakker said "don't touch that dial, there's someone out there in a motel room getting ready to commit suicide." The pilot went on to say his brother was now saved and serving as an elder in his church.'

****

On one of our trips my wife and I met Wendy Fast, a young girl who had sold her horse, moved from West Virginia with hopes of becom-ing a PTL singer. She was, at that time, a waitress in Morrison's Cafeteria and also had a part in the Passion Play. For several trips we were blessed with her exuberance and vibrant personality. On one occasion we invited Wendy to a restaurant off the grounds. While having lunch she blessed us with this story: She said "I don't know how you will receive this and nothing like this has ever happened to me before." She lived in Rock Hill and had made a close friend when she first came to PTL. Her friend had been diagnosed with a painful form of leukemia. One night she was going home from her friend's house and was suddenly impressed to return and stay with her through the night. During the night he friend rose up in bed anguishing in pain. Wendy, torn and frustrated that she could do nothing to ease her friend's pain, cried out to God asking Him to please help her friend. As she did, in her desperation, the back of her hand touched her friend's forehead. Her friend instantly fell back to the pillow. Wendy thought she was dead. Then she realized a peace had settled over her friend. She slept peacefully the remainder of the night. The next visit to her doctor, he could find no trace of leukemia. (Wendy Fast's last known address: Route 1, Box 278A, Fairmont, WV 26554).

****

At the end of a Marilyn Hickey service, my daughter Judy, went forward and God healed her knee. Problem solved! Marilyn asked everyone who wanted their finances healed to hold up their wallets and Judy's husband, John raised his high. Within a year they had moved from Buffalo, NY to Delaware and their income had doubled.

****

This story came from Aunt Susan and needs to be clarified:
Uncle Henry spoke in tongues on the PTL TV program and was dressed down pretty severely by those in charge. (That was before anyone dared to do such a thing on television). Some time later, He and Susan were invited to speak at a church (I think in the mid-west). Their plane was late which made them anxious about getting to the church on time. As they rushed down the aisle an elderly man grabbed Henry's arm. In broken English he said "I saw you on television, speaking in my native tongue and I was saved."

Paige S. Orange
3 York Way
Hockessin, De 19707-1343
302-239-3203

Ray in Front of Toy Shoppe

Grand Hotel

Entrance to Grand Hotel

Viola VanderLinde has not been in this area long, but as you can tell from her letter, she has found many riches in the form of friends and neighbors. Everyone was willing and happy to help her in any way they could when she was in need of transportation after an accident involving her automobile. She has found unusual friendship and offers of assistance.

Dear Reader,
My home town is Grand Rapids Michigan. I've been overseas in South America doing missions' work for the English people. We prayed a year for workers to come together and have an outreach ministry in a hotel for the upper class. There aren't any missionaries to the upper class in Chili. There are for the Spanish, but not any for the English people. I was involved in a fellowship for the missionaries and did a Bible study. It was kind of ministering to the people who didn't have anyone. They had a church, but they didn't know about being born again.

The pastor was from New Zealand. I was there and another from the United States. I was there for four years, but broke my hip and had to come back. I have only been to Heritage since July 1997 except to visit. When I visited before, I found the grounds and the lights to be beautiful, but the one thing that struck me as we were leaving the grounds, my husband said "this is a little bit like heaven until you get there." He wasn't talking about the grounds or the buildings, but about the friendly people and the love. We went to the Upper Room and to seminars afterwards, but I had never stayed on the grounds until I came this time.

Now that I'm living on the grounds and meeting the people who lived here and who had to go through the pain and embarrassment of what happened here. I am here writing and have only met a few people walking or associating and they have really ministered to me during this time. Through it all, God is still ministering through these people and their love. I know that I could call two or three of the people here at any time and tell them if I needed anything,

and they'd come. Today, I'm writing a book on breaking the ties that bind, breaking Satan's hold on people.
Viola VanderLinde

Paulette James found gems of unmeasurable value at P.T.L. in the recreational facilities, the safe envirnoment and the friendships that were so easily formed. Without having to go to a trinket shop, the children found treasures.

Dear Reader,
The first time I came to P.T.L. was in the '80's with my two children. We watched P.T.L. on television and they kept advertising the water park. So we were on our way to Myrtle Beach and we stopped. The boys had a wonderful time. In fact, they didn't want to go on to the beach. We were impressed with the shops and the beauty and especially with the feeling about the place.

We went on to the beach, but they wanted to come back. So we came back and stayed. I was a single mom, and I felt so safe with my boys here, safe and secure. There was such a different feeling.

I was attending a nondenominational church before I came here. My husband and I after we met and were married, came here for our honeymoon. It's always been a really special place to us. We attended the seminars and workshops. We found a feeling here that we'd never found anywhere else.

We just keep coming back and hoping that things will be back the way they were. We brought a group of people from our church here, rented two chalets and had a ball. I see the beginning of a new ministry for this place.
Paulette James

Virginia McCullum and her family purchased a time share at P.T.L. and as you can tell from her letter, found riches untold of peace and understanding which they took away to pass on to others today.

Dear Reader,

I first came to P.T.L. around 1982 or 1983, three nights and four days in the Grand Hotel. We had heard them on television and sent in our membership for the Grand Hotel. We loved it and sort of grew up with P.T.L. as it grew. The hotel was luxury with every convenience for the Partners. We came each year, bringing our children later on. We felt like it was God's property and His place and had the feeling that we were HOME. My husband said, I want our children to feel the feeling I feel when I'm on this property. So we rented one of the chalets and brought three of our four children and grandchildren on Easter weekend. We went to the broadcasts and kept busy hearing the wonderful Bible teachers and gospel singers.

My daughter said she didn't worry about her children while she was on the grounds. My husband volunteered in the mailroom and we went to all the seminars we could get in. We got such valuable teaching. We heard Judy Chevez and other wonderful man from Scotland. The dinner theaters were so wonderful.

When the news came out about Jim, our pastor Ron said, "But for the grace of God, there go I." In April, my husband was diagnosed with leukemia. He was in remission for three months and we came for our last visit to the grounds together. He went to the Upper Room and had Uncle Henry pray for him. That meant so much for him. We loved him so much and all of his hugs. We increased in knowledge from the wonderful preaching and teaching. We were entertained in the most Christian way by the different singers, etc.

When they reopened the Grand Hotel, my daughters, granddaughters and I came back for a visit. We saw that the time shares were available. I wanted my granddaughters to see the fall leaves so I talked about buying a time share so we could come the second week in November when the leaves were in full color. My sons have come down. My sister and her daughter have come. Everyone just loves the area and we always have a good time.

Words can never tell what P.T.L. and Heritage U.S.A. has meant to me and part of my family because of the rich teaching by very spiritual Christian people that I was able to sit under because of P.T.L. and because of this place. It was such a time of rest and relaxation and growing in the Lord that you couldn't experience any other place. No other resort area had any Christian influence, but here at Heritage you had the spiritual Christian influence, I couldn't have received any other place.

Virginia McCullum

Doris Havens is a shining example of the good that came from P.T.L. She praises God for all the treasures that were mined at P.T.L. and tells of the way God poured out (and continues to pour out) His blessings.

I met Jim & Tammy Bakker in the early 60's. They came to Wilmington, N.C. to hold a meeting in our church - First Assembly. Jim preached. Tammy played the piano. Every one fell in love with them - such a cute couple. My husband took Jim deep sea fishing. They got some big ones.
In 1980 we starting watching P.T.L. program every morning at 6 am. Liked it so well we decieded to visit Charlotte & atend the T.V. program. They had a two hour program on Park Rd. I worked on the prayer phones some. Decieded to move here we liked it so well. Sold my home in Wilmington and moved here & lived in a mobile home for a couple years. They were building homes here. So did move in Dogwood Hills in 1982. After my husband past away with a heart attack. In 1984 I met my present husband at the Upper Room. He was from Canada on his way to Fla. He had been raised Catholic, but was. Born Again - I told him about the Holy Spirit - He recieved it in the Upper Room. He came here because of

Watching PTL. His name is the same as my son-in-law - First & Last. After a year's courtship we decided to get married - Have had a wonderful 11 years together. Praise God for this beautiful place. What a vision God gave Jim.

Lots of people came to Heritage & was saved. I prayed for lots of people on the phones. One man was fixing to take his life. After prayer he didn't. Many were healed of all kinds of sickness. Mat 18-19 says if two agree whatever we ask shall be done.

Praise God for all the good things that happened here. They out number the bad. I was a Charter Member of the church here. Big crowds came. God poured out his blessings. The word did go forth. Souls was saved - To God be the glory

Doris Havens
2790 Dogwood Hills Ct.
Fort Mill, S.C. 29715

In interviewing Yvonne Moore and her family, I found the essence of what coming to these grounds meant to so many people. They came because they were blessed of God. Neither they nor their children will ever forget the rich blessings that became theirs at P.T.L.

November 1997

Felix and Yvonne Moore began watching PTL Television Network in 1976. We became partners for over ten years 1976 – 1987.

We were blessed so much by Christian T.V. and became hungry and thirsty for God's Word. I asked for a copy of the open Bible "PTL Partner Edition" and for the first time in my life I began to study and draw closer to Jesus. Answer to Prayer.

In 1981 we went on vacation to a place called Heritage USA, a wonderful place for the family to enjoy. Our daughter Rene' was 11 years old. We live in Warner Robins, GA, soon after we spent more time there, because it was a special place dedicated to God. Everyday there was Prayer Preaching, Teaching, Singing, Souls Saved God is Good! Praise His Holy Name.

Since 1995 we take our five grandchilden on summer vacation. They love to go. "A place of Refuge"

I feel shelterd in the arms of God and children need a place on this earth today where they feel protected against harm.

"To God Be the Glory"

Love,
Yvonne Moore

Jim and Barbara Kirk know what it is to follow the leading of God totally in their lives. Through their problems they learned to depend on God. They have never given up trusting God because of the love and ministries they found at P.T.L.

Dear Reader,

Barbara and I were inspired to come to P.T.L. from central Pennsylvania. It happened in a very unexpected way. As I watched the program, on occasion we had sent a contribution, and I asked one time when they called, what type of businesses were here at P.T.L. I told them that I owned a Radio Shack store. The person said, "Oh, we don't have anything like that here. Maybe we could use a store like that." That sparked an idea that maybe God would lead us in that direction.

Then one evening when I was watching the program, Jim Bakker indicated that they were looking for additional stores. That gave me the inspiration that we were to be part of that. The next morning, I told my wife that I had felt we were to possibly go to be part of P.T.L.

We started packing the next day. We did it in faith. Until the very day that we moved, we were still packing. I decided we'd better check the place out and make sure it is what we thought it was. The children stayed in the day care while we took in the sights and programs available at the time. We checked out the stores on Main Street. They were all full. We went back with the definite inspiration that this was what we needed to do.

When we checked into the details of moving, we found that my agreement with Radio Shack was that I could "relocate my store in a mall." Accidently the attorneys had left out where the mall would be or when I could do the relocation, so I went to the regional vice president and told him I'd like to relocate my store -- in another location. He said I couldn't do that, but because they had neglected to say where the mall would be or when I could relocate so they relocated my store without any expense to me at all.

We traveled back and forth from our home in Shelby to Heritage Church and to different functions. My wife be-

came involved in the Girl's Home, helping out, and was hired at the Day Care Center as a teacher.

The manager of the hotel gave me a call one day and said a store location was going to be available. I told him I was definitely interested in that location. I went to my company and told them I would like to relocate in Heritage with a franchise. We were so happy to see God follow through with what we felt He had led us to do. We were still living in Shelby even after we began operating the store. The hotel gave me a room for $16.00 a night, but that began to add up to too much. When I told them I couldn't afford that, they gave me a bunk house to live in for weeks at no charge. My wife and children would come on the weekends to stay with me.

Whenever the place reopened, we decided to risk going back again. God closed the place because of Hurricane Hugo, we didn't fail. We walked around to get a feel for the place again. It felt like home.

We have gotten to know people who have a real heart for God, and a lot of those people still live here. Most of them say, I gave my money, not to buy something, but I gave to the Lord, and we got our money's worth. They still love it when the come back, they feel sad to see so many changes, but they still know it is God's place. You have so much more an opportunity to bring up counseling or witnessing even in your store in a place like Heritage U.S.A. because everything is so open.

Moving here has strengthened us spiritually and helped us grow in the Lord. Customers have ministered to us as much as we have ministered to them. God tells some of the customers things to tell me. Once two pastors came in, talked to me, held my hand, prayed with me, ministered to me. They didn't know me at all, but they cared.

One customer asked me if he could pray for my store, and two or three weeks later, he called back and said he'd felt inspired to call and let me know that my business was still in his prayers. God works things out and makes things possible. We do our best to accommodate our customers, but we are here for the Lord. God is still a part of this place, He's always been a part of this place, and He's going to restore this place.

If this place is shut down, we'll just ask God what He wants us to do next. God has directed us here through us praying and asking him what to do. We're not concerned about the future. WE know he'll do more than provide for us in ways we could never have dreamed. We thank God he gave us the opportunity to be a witness for him. A minister came in one day and told me I sense God has something special for you, something you've never experienced before. And he will be able to use your talents in business like you never thought you would. So we continue to look toward God's guidance. In the end, it is all for God's glory.

Jim and Barbara Kirk

Olive Richardson is today moving into the ministry because of the way she was touched by God at P.T.L. She found treasures in the Upper Room and in working with people on the telephones that shine through her ministries to God and His people today.

Dear Reader,

I first came to P.T.L. in 1986. I was a Financial Analyst for the Nestle company traveling all around. I loved my job and am very people oriented. I had always wanted to go to Jerusalem and had the opportunity to go. While there on the Mount of Olives, another participant on the trip invited me to come to P.T.L. She was very excited about P.T.L. She was full of the love of God, you could see it and feel it in her.

So I came. I don't know what I was expecting. I did a lot of traveling and was used to places and people, but it was totally above what I had expected. I think it was because you could feel the presence of God here when you entered. The lady who invited me was such a wonderful anointed person of God. She had a studio apartment in a lakeside cabin. I'd see her in the morning, reading the Bible, raising her hands and praising God silently so she wouldn't disturb me.

Going to the Upper Room and walking those steps with the scripture on them was very rewarding. Everyone was so friendly. It seemed like we were all together praising God. I was invited to work on the telephones when we'd go to the studio for the television program. There was so much here then and I was getting so much out of it that I finally decided I needed to give them some time. The gentlemen thought I had already worked the phones, so he thought I knew what I was doing. Everything was color coded. "If you have a problem, just call the supervisor," he said. A young lady called Karen called, "She'd had enough and wanted to commit suicide." We talked and prayed and when we finished praying things were well with Karen. The Lord worked through the situation. Then the next call came, an alcoholic and the next a job situation. When I finished the day, I asked if I could come back the next day and the next. I spent the rest of my time on the phones. There was such a need out there.

When I left this place I was crying all the way home, "Lord, I need more time for you. What can I do?" And when I got home there was a phone call from one of the ladies I worked with. We were friends on the job and she'd called to tell me that anyone of a certain age could take early retirement. I found out when I went in, I could retire that December, right away almost, or take six months and wait until next June. I decided to wait until June. I had 130 sick days due me. But that whole 130 days, I didn't take a single sick day.

I began to wonder if I was doing the right thing. I called a friend who is a nun in Cincinnati and I called her and told her the story. "Olive," she said, "did you ask God for time?"

"Yes"
"Has he answered your prayer?"
"Why yes."
"What is your question, my dear?"

I never looked back.

There I was in my fifties and the Lord had led me to P.T.L. in strange ways. At my church, I was singing in a choir in New York City in Calvary Baptist Church. I had given up the singing because of my traveling. I had gone back to the church looking for Bible Study. For about seven months, I was asked by some ladies there to lead a Bible Study. I finally started a Bible study. I don't believe I would have ever done that if I hadn't gone to P.T.L. because I'd still have been too tied up with the work that I loved. As a result of that, I went down to College of New Rochelle and studied Christian Education and then to a seminary. I received my masters all in preparation for teaching.

Today I am moving into the ministry. My pastor has given me permission to do my trial sermon. I can see the hand of God in the way he moved me to Jerusalem and hearing about P.T.L. on the Mount of Olive, and strangely moving me with those telephone conversations.

The Bible says, "think it not strange when fiery trials come upon you." So we have to be strong in our focus. He says, "If my people who are called by my name will humble themselves and pray and turn from their wicked ways, seek my face, then I will come in, I will forgive their sins and heal the land." He says to seek my face, who I am.

Olive Richardson

Mary Simmons is the daughter of Vivian Jones, and as you read her letter, you will see that God still has a hand in the lives of individuals that were involved with P.T.L. Diamonds reappeared even brighter than before.

Dear Reader,

Brother Richard Dortch is my neighbor in Florida now. Before he became my neighbor this time two years ago, God put him in my path as a counselor though a very emotional time in my life, a time of a divorce and the death of my son. So Brother Dortch has really touched my heart and my life very deeply. He has shared things with me as he has with multitudes of people though his books and television programs. I love him and Mildred.

I didn't know him here on the grounds, not until after he had left here. I met him by providence of God back in 1988. He began to share with me then and as our lives have interlocked even more after he came out of prison about a prophecy that was given maybe two weeks before he had to give up. He came into a service one Sunday morning and said, you know how it is when you get in a church service and someone comes out with a message in tongues. We have gotten so used to it that you begin to wonder if's the flesh. This particular morning your little mother came out with a message in tongues and the interpretation. It probably wasn't for anyone there but me. If was God speaking totally for me, preparing my heart for what I knew was going to be exposed. If was so on target for my life that I contacted my secretary. I want you to go back and copy that off the Sunday morning's tape and to this day I have it sitting in a frame on my desk. God used Mother and she had no idea of this.

Mary Simmons

I became acquainted with Teresa Moore at Aunt Susan's home during the services that Judy Chevez leads for those on the grounds. Teresa and her husband began a ministry in the mountains of Virginia serving people in need with clothes, food and other necessities. This is a tremendous ministry and one that Teresa continues today even after the death of her husband.

Dear Reader,

My husband, Bob, was in the air force for 21 years, so we traveled all over before settling in the mountains of Virginia. I came here in 1990. I know it was the Lord's work moving us here. I have a ministry called Feeding His Lambs Ministry. I go into the mountains of Tennessee, Kentucky, Virginia, West Virginia, and the Cherokee Indian Nation to take food, clothing, and the gospel.

We moved to Charlotte after P.T.L. closed to find work,

but we had been coming down to P.T.L. from the time it was opened. The Lord kept drawing us here. We felt the Holy Spirit each time we'd come. Bob was president of the association and handled any problems that came up.

I remember the time David Wilkerson was here. I had low blood sugar and had gone to the doctor. They told me what to eat and what not to eat, but I didn't really want to do it. I knew the Lord could heal me at the right time. When we came to hear David Wilkerson, he said, "There are people here with low blood sugar and they are being healed ..." and he asked us to stand up. I stood up, and from that point on, I've never had a problem.

I first heard about P.T.L. from my daughter-in-law. I was having trouble with arthritis and she said, I couldn't sleep last night, and I turned on the television and head this man. You might want to hear it." So the next night, I turned it on. I can't remember the exact words Jim said, but he said something like, "if you need a healing, I want you to focus on Jesus ... and get everything else out of your mind." I looked into the corner where there was nothing to distract me. And all of a sudden a light came on. I don't know what happened, but I sat there and when I looked at the clock again it was 2:00 a.m. I had been a Christian, but I knew there was something missing, but from that moment on I was filled with the Holy Spirit and by June I no longer had arthritis.

We wanted to live at P.T.L. so badly, but we couldn't afford a place. Bob knew about the Lord, but he didn't know the Lord -- and neither of us believe he would have been ready to meet the Lord if we hadn't come to P.T.L. God is still here.

I worked on the prayer phones. I had my little counselor's Bible there in front of me and whatever their need was, I looked for it under that category and read it over and over to them and talked to them about it.

I feel like this place will rise again. I feel like what is happening now is a total death, and there can't be a resurrection until there's a death. The bad, the old, whatever has passed away will be dead shortly, and when it's dead, God

will resurrect it and it will be the most wonderful place to come -- better than before -- to the glory of God.
Teresa Moore

Jan Johnson was an employee of the hotel who showed great strength of character even though she lost the position which she loved. Her faith in God strengthened her to the point where she knew that God would supply all her needs. She has today found another position and continues to spread diamonds wherever she goes.

Dear Reader,

Years and years ago, I lived in Alabama. I never watched P.T.L. television. I just wasn't interested. I remember my niece and her husband were so excited about going to P.T.L. for a marriage retreat. I thought they needed to spend their money at the beach. When they came back, they were so excited, but I still thought, I would never go there.

But I have ended up living here, working here and having a great appreciation for the ministry that went on here. I was living in Tega Cay doing interior design work. I answered the job fair ad. The place had been shut down for two years then. There were about 60 people in line. I put my application in and in about 10 minutes they called me in to talk about a position.

When I first started working here, I was in so many different areas. In the Hall of Faith, there were large frames with names of people who had contributed. I was awestruck by all those little tiny brass plaques. A week or so later I came back in and those frames with those little plaques were just dropped in huge piles. I went over and picked up names and looked at it and knew that person had personally invested in this place and knowing that there were thousands of those people's names under there.

I've been here at the hotel for five ½ years doing seven different jobs. It has been a great experience and through each of the avenues I've had personal experiences where my growth has grown to a huge broad spectrum of understanding. Personally what happened to me -- my exposure to all

Main Street

The Train That Traveled Around the Lake

the different faiths who walked though these doors - it became very apparent to me that each of the different ways of worshiping Christ came though these doors -- I had a very narrow view of what Christ expected form us -- but I was challenged as to how God wants us to think about him.

One day an international group Pentecostal holiness group was in. These people at one table were from South America. We were having a great moment, very joyful, but after the group left, a man from the table came up to me and said, you don't know what you just did. These people come from a country where sharing faith openly is very dangerous and for someone to come up so openly and share their faith with them took them totally off guard because they weren't used to it. We had a moment of prayer. He said, "You know, right now you are in a green house and God will grow you. One day there will be a time for you to go out."

That was one of a hundred moments that happened here. People tend to think, "Ah, it's closed. It's not P.T.L. any more." I don't know what it was like before, but I can tell you this -- the groups that come through this door -- it's still there-- lives are still changed. People don't see it, because it's not only the national news -- reports in the paper are not going to tell you how an individual life has changed and grown. It's an individual experience that people come, have, and go away with -- and I had that experience to be able to tell Jim last New Years Eve.

I was completely alone in this hotel once and there was one lady who came up to me-- and she said, "I just want to . . . " and she walked away. Then she came back and said, "I just need to talk to somebody." And for that moment, my time was hers. I had gone through separation and divorce and lost everything. Yet through that time of my life, all my needs were met, not abundant, but my needs were met. We prayed and we cried, and she left. And I knew that was what was so important -- that we can reach them through the masses with the television shows -- but one on one it the way it happens.

I was in the cafeteria one day, very tired, my feet hurt. People were banging on the door, and I didn't' want to answer it. He banged again, so I went to answer the door. This little Mexican man peeked his head in - and asked for Jim. I told him Jim was in jail. He said, "Oh my wife and I we used to watch Jim, and we came to know the Lord because of this ministry. And then we had to move back to Mexico, but I always promised my wife that I would bring her back to the place that was responsible for this change in our lives.

"Please come in," I told him. "Walk these halls. Take your wife through." They came in, we had a moment of prayer and they went on. This showed me that there were still people even years later.

I used to give an orientation for the employees here at the hotel. We'd do a tour and stop by the Upper Room, the most special place on the property. My philosophy is that if someone needs prayer, that is the moment to pray. In the Upper Room, we heard about the Upper Room, but there was one employee who couldn't leave, she was in such need. I had no problem that if the one needed to stay, Pete and I prayed with her and hugged her and cried. This bonded that employee and me in a very spiritual way. Things like that continued to happen.

There was a banquet and in the room there were heads of different denominations all gathering together to discuss common elements of the curriculum. The leader said, "Take a look at this room, all these denominations, this is the first time ever that they have been together under one room. It was God breaking down the barriers. There is a commonality in Christ. We are the colors of the rainbow.

I went through the most difficult period of my life, but most people had no idea that any of that was happening to me, because people were led in the spirit to encourage me -- even people I didn't know would come up to me on the street and speak words of encouragement that helped me get through one more day. At each turn in my life, there were more personal provisions in time when I didn't know what the next move or moment would be.

I was getting ready to leave. It was after my first year and they wanted to move me to the restaurant. I had the three top gentlemen in the room and I was getting ready to tell them I was quitting, but someone knocked on the door and interrupted -- we've got some V.I.P.'s coming over to the headquarter building and they're going to have a high level meeting, we've got to take over a refreshment break for them. I agreed to help them, but I was thinking this is the last thing I'm going to do.

Suddenly I find myself in Dr. Coo's office, setting up refreshments and in walks Pat Robertson and his son and they're having a discussion. I think what am I doing standing here in this room with these men? Then we had to have a meal ready for them. It was nice, served well, the food was beautiful and everything went well. Then I turned to my employer, we talked, negotiated and came to an equitable agreement.

An interesting thing happened to me the week before the hotel closed. A car pulled in front of me and I hit her. She pulled her car back and I pulled my car off the side of the road. I got out of the car and went over to her, and there was no damage to her car. Then I went back and looked at the front of my car and there was not a scratch. "This is crazy. I know I hit you and this does not make sense." We exchanged numbers and off she went. I knew God had a lesson for me in that. That was on a Thursday before the Monday that they announced the closing.

When Monday's announcement came that the hotel would close I clearly started to feel that God had impressed on my heart, "you know, Jan, it looks like a wreck. It feels like a wreck. It should be a wreck, but it's not. So in the midst of this storm, I know that it looks like a closing, it feels like a closing, it should be a closing, but yet, God is with us through all this. There is a great sense of peace in the believers here. No one knows what's going to happen. We are looking for jobs, moving on with our lives, but there's a great sense of peace.

Jan Marie Johnson

Chapter **14**

REMEMBRANCE RING

A Treasure House Of Magnificent Moments and Memories

Matthew 13:44 reminds us that *"The kingdom of heaven is like unto treasure hid in a field; the which when a man hath found, he hideth, and for joy thereof goeth and selleth all that he hath, and buyeth that field."* My sincere desire is that this book might help us to realize how truly precious is the spreading of God's Word.

This chapter is truly a treasure house of magnificent moments and memories as we are reminded of the different kinds of jewels that were found at P.T.L., and the marvelous array of diamonds that are still being mined today.

First, I would like to share with you a poem by Reverend Rex E. Faile, Sr. which expresses everything I feel and everything I have tried to bring to you in this book:

A DIAMOND IN THE ROUGH

Sometimes I may not glitter or reflect my Lord's good grace,
Meeting man's approval with no times of disgrace.
Just know that God's not finished, and until He's said enough,
Keep the vault of heaven open, I'm still a diamond in the rough.

Though my value's not yet seen, and some would simply toss away,
There's a tree which stands on Calvary
that has another thing to say.
For the worth that Jesus saw when he gave his blood for us,
Said, "I finally found my jewel," a precious diamond in the rough.

While this gem does not yet show every facet of God's grace,
One day with his reflection, I'll see him face to face.
In his hand I am secure, blessed with every tender touch,
God makes a perfect stone of beauty from this diamond in the rough.

To those with hearts of coal, let me say to you today,
Take not this word for granted because there is a judgment day.
Yield your life to Him that's able and will change you by his love.
He'll take that worthless piece of coal and make
a diamond in the rough.

Rev. Rex E. Faile, Sr.

I feel so blessed to know God has had His hand on this book and all the people involved. I know that He has particularly had His hand on His "Special Children", the *GLORIOUS GEMS*, with whom we began the book. Matthew 19:13-15 tells us *"Then were there brought unto him little children, that he should put his hands on them, and pray: and the disciples rebuked them. But Jesus said, Suffer little children, and for-*

bid them not, to come unto me: for of such is the kingdom of heaven. And he laid his hands on them and departed thence."

Kim Lunsford was another beautiful young lady who came into our store. A pretty young coed from Troy State University, Kim was involved in a car accident in which her spinal cord was severed. Kim says, "I have a daily walk with God and our relationship grows stronger every day . . . if you put your faith in God, other things will fall into place. We never know what will happen tomorrow, and we should always be prepared."

While Kim was in the hospital, her mother tells us, "she was truly born again. This came about through Christian television broadcasts, especially Jim Bakker and P.T.L., Oral Roberts, and the Kenneth Copeland ministries." Kim claims Romans 8:28 as her scripture verse: *"And we know that all things work together for good to them that love God, to them who are called according to his purpose."*

Kim and her parents believe that God allowed her to live for a purpose. "I've given myself to the Lord," Kim says. "Whatever He wants me to do, I'll obey and do what He sees fit. I just thank God that He has opened the doors and given me the opportunity to share with others in my church and around the world."

Kim's parents would bring her into Noah's Toy Shoppe and wheel her around on a narrow bed. When I'd notice her eyes sparkling over a particular toy, I would somehow manage to place it on her bed where she'd find it later. Kim's parents bring us up to date in the following letter:

Dear Reader,

Hello from the Lunsford family. Our daughter, Kim, is a quadriplegic due to a car accident in 1982. At the times we visited Heritage USA, she used a phrenic pacemaker to breathe. Since then, she has had nerve damage to the phrenic nerves and cannot use it any longer. She is now ventilator dependent. We are able to use the pacemaker to suction but it only works on one lung. She has not been able to travel during the past few years, and has not been out of her bed in four years.

She is not depressed or bored however. The Lord has been good and she has a computer and the latest equipment at her disposal. She is the Executive Director of the HandiCAPABLE Challenge which offers respite care for families with a disabled family member and helps organizations and individuals receive necessary grants. They also help locate children with disabilities at as early an age as possible.

We met wonderful Christian people on every trip we made to P.T.L., both employees and visitors. The presence of God was certainly felt there. We stayed at other places as nice materially as Heritage USA, but no other place had the Christian fellowship that we found there.

The presence of the Lord was felt in the people. Prayer was prevalent at any point in time or any place you might be on the grounds. Whether you were shopping, at the dinner theaters or in the church services, you knew the people loved God. Kim felt at home and was not stared at, but prayed for. The presence of God in every activity was what was so unusual about Heritage.

One special person that we met and loved at P.T.L. was "Mr. Noah", who is of course, Ray Walters, the author of this book. God never made a finer man than him. I wish I could name others, but I'm sure I would forget someone, so I won't. Kim is designing a new web page for the City of Troy, Alabama, our home town now. She is enjoying the work immensely. So in the not too distant future, look up Troy on the Internet, and you will see Kim's work. Who knows, she might even convince you to come to Troy, to visit or maybe to live.

May God bless each and every reader of this book and heal those who were hurt by the downfall of P.T.L. and its leaders. We are all human and we can and do make mistakes. It is God's will that we forgive others so that He can forgive us.

The Lunsford Family

In Chapter Two we learned about the *PRECIOUS PRAYER* that went on in the Upper Room. Psalms 9:9-10 states, *"The Lord also will be a refuge for the oppressed, a refuge in times of trouble and they that know thy name will put their trust in thee; for thou, Lord, hast not forsaken them that seek thee."* Psalm 32:7 continues, *"Thou art my hiding place, thou shalt preserve me from trouble; thou shalt compass me about with songs of deliverance."*

The Upper Room served communion to thousands and thousands of Christians. Yes, it was indeed a place of refuge for those in need of prayer and a place of quiet where they could pour out their hearts to God. It was one of the richest mines of diamonds and treasures.

Mark 14:15-16 and 22-25 tells us, *"...He will shew you a large upper room furnished and prepared: there make ready for us. And his disciples went forth, and came into the city, and found as he had said unto them: and they made ready the Passover." "And as they did eat, Jesus took bread, and blessed, and brake it, and gave to them, and said, Take, eat; this is my body and he took the cup , and when he had given thanks, he gave it to them; and they all drank of it. And he said unto them, This is my blood of the new testament, which is shed for many. Verily I say unto you, I will drink no more of the fruit of the vine, until that day that I drink it new in the kingdom of God."*

Mary Alice Kelley tells us in the following letter about her healings in the Upper Room:

Dear Reader,

In August of 1987, I was diagnosed with low grade non Hodgkins Lymphoma - cancer in the fourth and final stage in the lymph nodes and bone marrow. I told my oncologist that I would not start chemo. I felt that if I could get to the Upper Room at P.T.L. and have them pray for me, I would be healed.

I've had many healings through my life. One was when I was run over by a truck in front of the Assembly of God Church in Tulsa, Oklahoma, when I was five years old. The truck drug me 20 feet. A physician was there and declared me dead, but on that Easter morning, they carried my body to the altar, interceding and crying out to God to spare my life. And the next day I was back in kindergarten.

At six years old, I was thrown through a car windshield and almost lost my eye. At seven, a gas oven exploded in my face and burnt off my hair, but didn't even scar my face. At twenty-five, after a hysterectomy which caused "surgical menopause", I began to have attacks where I would lapse into unconsciousness, almost paralyzed, and unable to speak or move. Later after a heart attack, I was fitted for steel braces for a deteriorating spine, and had hand surgery to replace the bones with plastic.

Once I almost choked to death when a foreign object from a fish dinner was lodged in my esophagus. Blood clots formed after another surgery. And then came the cancer. I can truly say that God sustained me during all those years. I knew that the God who had healed me before was still on the throne and he was not going to let Satan succeed this time either.

P.T.L. had been an important part of my life since I had begun watching it in 1980. I had gone back every year to spend two weeks there, and I knew of the miracles that could occur. I went to the Upper Room and had them pray for me, and three months after coming back home, the hospital did a bone marrow biopsy, checked the lymph nodes, and did blood work. They could not find a trace of cancer in my body.

The doctors said I truly had received a miracle of God. It has been ten years now, and they keep checking. They say the low-grade lymphoma always comes back, but when God heals, it's done right! So P.T.L. has been very special to me. I thank God for the many souls saved, healed, and delivered through that ministry. I was one, Praise God!

Mary Alice Kelley

All the different facets of Prison Ministry are covered in Chapter Four, *RADIATING RICHES*, and the one person who has had a hand in establishing and maintaining them is Jeff Park. Jeff is truly a man of God. During my visit with him to the state prison at Columbia for the Easter Sunrise Service,

I saw a man who was loved by all the prisoners. He is loved in prisons all over the United States and in other countries. There have been thousands of prisoners saved and nurtured back into society as a result of Jeff allowing God to work through him. The most tireless person I have ever met, his eyes and heart are on God as he continues God's work long after P.T.L. has closed. Thank you, Jeff Park!

The Bible tells us in Matthew 25:34-46, *"For I was an hungered, and ye gave me meat; I was thirsty, and ye gave me drink: I was a stranger, and ye took me in:Naked, and ye clothed me: I was sick, and ye visited me: I was in prison, and ye came unto me. Then shall the righteous answer him saying, Lord, when saw we thee an hungered, and fed thee? Or thirsty, and gave thee drink? When saw we thee a stranger, and took thee in? Or naked and clothed thee? Or when saw we thee sick, or in prison, and came unto thee? And the king shall answer and say unto them, Verily I say unto you, Inasmuch as ye have done it unto one of the least of these my brethren, ye have done it unto me. Then shall he say also unto them on the left hand, Depart from me, ye cursed, into everlasting fire, prepared for the devil and his angels; for I was an hungered, and ye gave me no meat, I was thirsty, and ye gave me no drink: I was a stranger, and ye took me not in: naked, and ye clothed me not: sick, and in prison, and ye visited me not. Then shall they also answer him saying, Lord, when saw we thee an hungered, or athirst, or stranger, or naked, or sick, or in prison, and did not minister unto thee? Then shall he answer them saying, Verily, I say unto you, Inasmuch as ye did it not to one of the least of these, ye did it not to me. And these shall go away into everlasting punishment: but the righteous into life eternal."*

Jeff says when men come out of prison, 37% of them are homeless. They have to go back on the streets. There is very little hope of a guy coming out with no home, no money, and no I.D. to get a job. That's why so many go back to crime during the first few weeks they are out of prison. Dogwood Manor, the re-entry home, grew out of Fort Hope. Jeff Park tells us, "When we lead someone to Christ in the jail, we disciple them, and those that have no place to go are invited to come to Dogwood Manor. We have more than 100 volunteers at the Moss Justice Center in York County and more than 200 volunteers in Charlotte. There are life skills programs for those who need them which focus on helping them receive the basic parenting understanding they should have received at home -- any thing from health issues to marriage. From drug and alcohol problems to vocational or financial issues, we try to teach the men how to live responsibly out there.

These programs are taught four hours a day in the jail system as a recovery program. Then we continue it in a more concentrated manner once they come to Dogwood Manor. This is just one of our several after-care programs.

God has called us to disciple and when we go into the prisons, we spend a little time with a lot of people, and a lot of time with the people we feel He has specifically given each of us. He has called us to be faithful and make disciples, so we begin with that end in view. We try to equip our volunteers to be prepared to disciple broken people. The goal is to build relationships with the men, then disciple them through the Word of God and testimony to Christ.

Fort Hope came about when I asked Jim if I could build a center on the land across the railroad tracks from the Farm. I wanted it to be a place to help take men off the street who were just out of prison. It was designed to house 120 men and teach them vocational training, spiritual foundation training, and disciplines -- the basic responsibilities of manhood. It was a place for men to be reparented who had never had a dad to teach them the ways of life. We dedicated Fort Hope on July 4, 1996. This required a significant financial contribution each month for staff, etc., so when the funding for P.T.L. ended, that facility closed.

Some of the staff and clients went from there to Rebound a program that is still going on. The director is now with the Teen Challenge Center in Cincinnati. And today we have Dogwood Manor right across the street where we house six men. One of the first men I discipled is now a chaplain and has one of the largest Christian ministries in North Carolina.

Fort Hope was, as you can see, one of the very important jewels found at P.T.L. Men like Jim Gray and Ken Davis played an essential role in that ministry to help teach and train the men in their reintroduction into society. Ken was the Vocational Coordinator for Fort Hope. It is obvious that God brought Ken to P.T.L. specifically to work with the men. From the following letter, you can tell how much the men meant to Ken and how much Ken meant to the men -- and how much both meant to God.

Dear Reader,

My wife, Priscilla, and I came to P.T.L. from my own consulting business in Albemarle, NC. We sold the business in 1981 and through some events where I came into the fullness of the Lord, I began to feel God's stirring. We moved to Huntersville, and in about six months, we ended up visiting and finally staying at P.T.L.

I was watching television one day when the concept of Fort Hope was brought up. I thought it was a wonderful idea and the next day I went and spoke to Jeff Park. I had already been volunteering for him in the prison ministry. We talked about Fort Hope and within a few months he hired me to be the vocational coordinator for the Fort.

The concept of Fort Hope was to bring guys in who had been struggling with drugs or alcohol or some other life debilitating condition and help them grow in the Lord and then to train them to take a productive role in society by learning how to work and develop job skills. We also worked with local industry and vocational rehabilitation for South Carolina in placing them.

I was learning from's God's word that he wanted to take the lids off His people and allow them to be free. I could see from working with the men that God had put tremendous potential in everybody. These men had been deeply wounded and had lids holding them down from being all that God wanted them to be. They couldn't be successful because of the bondages in their lives, and they could not rise above those bondages by themselves.

The Lord began to show me that He was using us to take lids off. I got up every day excited about seeing men's lives changed. It was like God had chosen each member of the staff, and we felt very privileged that God had chosen us to do this important work for Him. It was not only happening to the men, it was happening to each of us as well. We were changed in the process.

In a group of men, there would be several ones that I felt like God had assigned to me. One young man, who was an assignment of mine, wanted to learn how to do a specific job skill which was technical. I told the Lord I needed a good learning opportunity for that young man. In a few days a man showed up in my office from Ohio. He was a technical school instructor. He was working over at the Grand and he wondered if I had anyone he could train. I said, Yes, and put this young man with him. He graduated from the Fort, and went into that business.

Hebrews 4:12 says "The word of God is quick and powerful, and sharper than a two edged sword." We all know that God has the ability to be velvet when He needs to be and a sword when He needs to be. There were times with the men when the Word of God had to be spoken directly and truthfully and let it do the necessary surgery. There were times when we had to speak some pretty hard truths into the lives of the men, but it was God taking those lids off. Some of them bucked, and kicked and ran. Others bucked and kicked but realized that it was God working in them and that they had to stay and submit. The ones who submitted to God's Word were the ones who were successful.

One man went to Youth with a Mission, stayed three years, and met his wife. Now he is in computer school in Atlanta and growing and becoming who he was meant to be. Another man is ministering to people who are in prison. There was an article about him in Voice Magazine. There was another young man who had been on the streets of California in Skid Row for five years. He came to Fort Hope and then I got him into Bible College. We saw men getting direction in their lives. There were probably close to a hundred men who went through Fort Hope, but if there had only been one, it would have been worth it.

The men touched everyone in the ministry. I would take the men to give them an opportunity to testify about what God was doing in their lives. We went into different departments of the ministries and conducted devotions telling where they had been and where they were going.

I still remember when Fort Hope closed. We had twelve guys left in the Fort during those last few months. The Lord spoke to me one day in the staff meeting. These were a tremendous group of fellows all hungry for what God was doing in their lives, and yet everything was falling apart around them, but we were really seeing them stand in faith even though they were uncertain about their future.

We were planning to have a graduation for these guys. We had gotten all of them placed in different programs around the country or had some direction planned for them. That's when the Lord said to me, "I do not want you guys to go away from here with your heads hanging down. I want you to go out of here like a flame of fire." I told the director we needed to have the final graduation in the Grand Lobby and celebrate what God had done. He told me, he'd give me until 3:00 the following afternoon to see if I could pull it together.

The next day, one of the counselors in Fort Hope and I walked over to the Grand and found the gentleman who was in charge of the hotel. We told him we wanted to have a gradation in the lobby of the Grand, to serve dinner and really "put it on" for the men. "God told me we were to go out like a flame of fire!" I said to him. "We want the best you have, the court yard, a nice dinner served to the men, the staff, and their guests."

He agreed to do it all for $100.00. I gave $50.00, and everyone pooled their money for the rest. Uncle Henry was there with us, and Partners were standing around the two levels of the Grand looking over the balcony as we celebrated these last guys leaving Fort Hope.

The last day I was at the Fort, after all the guys had gone, and we had cleaned up and stored things, I was walking back down the road toward to Fort to pick up my things. I stopped and stood there in the road. "God," I said, "what is all this about?"

In my mind I saw this huge corn stalk that went straight

up in the air. "What happens to the stalk when the fruits have been picked?" the Lord asked.

"It dies," I said. And then I saw — the Fort was the stalk, the fruit were the men and the staff. The seed was in the fruit and God was scattering the seed. That settled it for me. I didn't have any more questions. He set me free that moment and helped me understand what was going on. I got my things and walked out of there and have been blessed by what he showed me that day ever since.

The Lord says in his word, that "unless a seed falls in the ground and dies, it won't bear fruit." This place had to die, but fruit is being born. I believe what he was telling me about Fort Hope was true for the whole ministry, that He was casting seed. It doesn't take much to see all the seed that was scattered out of this place of healing for me. I could see the hand of God. All the money, all the time, all the lives we sowed in the ministry were simply a gift to God and we have seen it returned many, many times over.

One day when I was driving past the main gate on my way home from work, the thought came to my mind that I'd like to go in and pray over the buildings. But I talked myself out of it and drove on to the house. Two months went by, and I met Earl Colson, who "just happened" to be the one with the keys to the buildings. I told him about my wish, and he agreed to meet me there one day.

We met over there one Sunday and went to the Upper Room first. Greass had grown up around it and a big chain was on the door. We walked up to the door, and I said, "In the name of Jesus, be loosed." And Earl unlocked the door, took the chain off and we went in. Before he and I could get into the center of the place, both of us had tears in our eyes and were thanking God for what he was doing. We stood in the center and prayed and told the Upper Room to come alive again.

We went to the amphitheater next, took the chains off the door, walked into the center of the place and slung olive all over and told it to come alive again. Those were the only two places the Lord told me to go to that day, and those two places have been revived. They were and are the heart of this place.

All that was reported about P.T.L. were the problems, but there were people that were touched by the power of God, people released from bondages and people who began to live fruitful lives because of Fort Hope and the other ministries. That can never be taken away from those of us who saw the depth of what went on at P.T.L.

We must look deeper than the surface. The seed falls in the ground and dies. Then comes the blade, the ear, the full corn in the ear, and then the harvest. When that seed dies in the ground new life is already in that seed. We must be patient and let the light in, and soon whatever is in that seed will break through the ground and grow, first the blade, then the ear, and then the full corn.

Ken Davis

In the next letter, Jim Gray tells us about a young woman that he and the other workers helped to overcome drug addiction:

Dear Reader,

I am glad that my "cowboy friend" out in Colorado introduced me to the Fort Hope Ministry after he met Jesus while watching the P.T.L. television program one cold frosty morning. The following story is only one of many that I saw in the two short years I worked at Fort Hope.

Friday afternoon had finally arrived and the warm afternoon sun was streaming through the window into my office at Fort Hope on the grounds of beautiful Heritage USA. The men on the program were doing great. Most were contemplating a laid back weekend of fishing and church on Sunday with hundreds of visitors over in the big barn.

The voice of my secretary on the intercom jolted me back to reality. "Jim, there's a troubled young lady here to see you... says her name is Cora Lee and you are expecting her. She appears to be high and is very impatient and belligerent."

This girl lived five hours away and had nearly driven me to exhaustion over the past several weeks with phone calls all hours of the day and night. I assured her that God loved her and that our ministry was committed to helping hurting people like her.

Cora Lee told me that she ran with a gang of girls who were all dying a slow death from drugs and alcohol. She had made contact with us through the P.T.L. television show. When she called, she was recognized as a serious case and referred to our counseling department at Fort Hope. I had encouraged her to visit us at Heritage for a few days so we could pray in the Upper Room. And now here she was outside my office on a balmy Friday afternoon.

I caught up with her just as she swore another oath and ran out the door dragging a kid with her. When I stopped her in the parking lot, filthy language poured out of her like a river, and one look into those dancing hollow eyes spoke a thousand words into my spirit. Demons were having a hay day with this girl. Her very life was being destroyed.

I left her three-year-old son with my son and his wife, and called our ministry team of three ladies and four men who were street wise and trained in spiritual warfare. Watching Cora Lee kick drugs was as ugly as I remembered from my many years on staff with Teen Challenge. Add the demonic influence deeply embedded inside the poor girl, and you've got an experience you don't want to see without being saturated in God's compassion and grace. She had the strength of two men and blasphemed God and us with every breath. We prayed and ministered Christ's love to her for 48 hours solid. She finally came to herself and began praising God for His love and mercy.

We didn't know that this was just Round One of what would be an ongoing fight to save this girl and her child's life. Just two weeks after she returned home, my wife, Naomi, opened our door to find a very sick Cora Lee and her child. Cora Lee collapsed in the hallway and little Ricky began to scream. Needless to say, my phone rang at Fort Hope. In the next 24 hours the demons cursed God through Cora Lee's child. He had many fits of violence and terror, even hitting me in the nose twice in the same night. Eventually as I held a pillow between us and prayed for him, deliver-

ance came and he slumped into my arms with a very welcome bear hug. Cora Lee stayed in our home for the next 14 days as the withdrawal tore at her body.

After she went home this time, the third and final round came. She called me, screaming into the phone, "The girls are going to kill me! Please come and get me!" My wife and I grabbed a flight out of Charlotte, kidnaped Cora Lee and her child, and brought them to the sanity and safety of Heritage USA. Her husband came looking for her and ended up asking for our help also. We provided a trailer for them near Fort Hope, and they stayed there for nine months while he worked at a job in Rock Hill. They stayed in the area for another year before moving back to their home state.

We have had many visits from Cora Lee since, and I'm always blessed when I hear Ricky say, "I love you Uncle Jim!" Would Cora Lee be alive today without the ministry of Heritage? What about Ricky who is 14 years old now and doing fine? Was it worth the time and money? How will this story play in eternity? Only God knows the answers to my questions!

Jim Gray

Chapter Five, GOLDEN GLITTERS, tells us about the P.T.L. Centers that were started in churches. There were probably 800 People That Love Centers which opened all over the country. The Centers were intended from the beginning to be associated with local churches, so when P.T.L. closed, the Center that was located on the grounds moved to Faith Assembly Church in Rock Hill. It is still operating there today and people are won to Christ through that outreach every month.

Many of the Centers are still operating as outreaches of local churches. One that is operating really excitingly in Charlotte is the one at the Community Outreach Church. Jeff Park, tells us about it in the following letter:

Dear Reader,

It has been the most exciting project that I've been involved with. As I mentioned earlier, this started in 1981 when Barbara Bruton came to the P.T.L. Center, weeping that her husband had been shot to death there. It was a place where police were afraid to go, and the church had been turned over to the black mafia. It was such a violent community the city had directed that a wall be built to separate it from the other homes. It was the third most violent community in America. There were deaths there every week and all kinds of violence.

Barbara was preaching on the edge of the community in her brother-in-law's garage, and the city was going to tear down the garage and build a parking lot, so she wanted P.T.L. to help start a P.T.L. Center.

We went into the area, brought the P.T.L. singers, played games with the kids, turned one of the buildings into a People That Love Center and in a couple of years, the church was taken back from the Mafia. A beautiful new building was built, and the community has now gone from the third worst violent community in the nation to the 41st worst in Charlotte. They have renamed all the streets good names like Peaceful Blvd and Holy Spirit Walkway. The whole community has been redone.

This is only one example of the communities where the Body of Christ is getting involved, and that is what works — Christians working hand in hand!

Jeff Park

Chapter Six, *SPLENDID SERVANTHOOD*, is aptly named for Henry Harrison. Uncle Henry loved everyone so much that I am certain he has a special place and assignment in heaven. When he was asked the reason why he was always so happy and upbeat, he answered, "ATTITUDE!"

"Attitude," he said, "has more impact on a situation than the situation itself!"

I John 4:6-10 teaches, *"We are of God: he that knoweth God heareth us; he that is not of God heareth not us. Hereby know we the spirit of truth, and the spirit of error. Beloved, let us love one another, for love is of God; and everyone that loveth is born of God, and knoweth God. He that loveth not knoweth not God; for God is love. In this was manifested the love of God toward us, because that God sent his only begotten Son into the world, that we might live through him. Herein is love, not that we loved God, but that he loved us, and sent his Son to be the propitiation for our sins."*

The telephone ministry in Chapter Seven, truly was a way of *WINNING WEALTH* for God. There is no way to tell how many souls were won for God through the telephone calls that came in. Matthew 16:27 says, *"For the son of man shall come in the glory of his Father with his angels; and then he shall reward every man according to his works."* There surely will be rewards for those dedicated servants of God who spent hours and hours praying and counseling with people over the phones. Lives were saved, marriages healed, ministries rebuilt, faith restored through one person simply talking to another person over the telephone lines and both of them talking to God.

In Chapter Eight, we learned about the *GLEAMING GIFTS*, the radio and television ministries. Mark 16:15 instructs us to *"Go ye into all the world, and preach the gospel to every creature. He that believeth and is baptized shall be saved; but he that believeth not shall be damned."* The radio and television ministries were the perfect vehicles to do that. They could not, however, have been effective without the people. The "people that loved" other people enough to reach out to them through these electronic marvels were the real soul savers. In the following letter, Eileen Swoda tells us about watching the television program and shares a poem she has written with us.

Dear Reader,
I used to get up at 5:00 a.m. every morning to watch P.T.L. on television. That was before they bought the land for Heritage. I actually love it here more now than when everything was going on. It's not so busy, and you have time to visit. You can feel the love here everywhere.
Eileen Swoda

A mighty task Jesus had you undertake,
but you willingly caught the sparkle for His sake.
Thanks for taking the journey -- seeing God's vision;
the gems in this book will heal much division.
Eileen Swoda

Through the section in Chapter Nine, called *JOYFUL JEWELS*, you have been made more aware of the ministries to birth mothers, adoptive parents and their babies. Adoptions were first mentioned in the Bible. In Exodus 2:10 we learn that the King's daughter adopted Moses, and Esther 2:7 tells us that Mordecai had raised Esther as his own daughter. We, ourselves, are adopted by God. Deuteronomy 14:1-2 tells us, *"... the Lord your God chose you to be his own. You belong to the Lord."* John 1:13 says, *"God himself was the one who made them his children."* And Romans 8:15 says, *"God's Spirit doesn't make us slaves who are afraid of him. Instead we become his children and call him our Father."* Galatians 4:3-7 agrees, *"That is how it was with us. We were like children ruled by the powers of this world. But when the time was right, God sent his Son, and a woman gave birth to him. His Son obeyed the Law, so he could set us free from the law and we could become God's children. Now that we are his children, God has sent the Spirit of his Son into our hearts. And his spirit tells us that God is our Father."* (Contemporary English Version - 1995, American Bible Society, NY).

The following letters from Jean Veckruise and Ann Ippolito are even more enlightening. Both were involved with the P.T.L. Home for Unwed Mothers and the Tender Loving Care Adoption Agency, and both are still involved today with the same services through Christian Family Services Adoption Services. As I listened to their stories, my heart jumped with gladness!

Dear Reader,

I came to P.T.L. from Louisiana State University School of Medicine where I worked in the medical school. The Lord led me very specifically. My life was in shambles at the time, and I was coming through Charlotte on the way back from visiting my mother in Buffalo, New York.

I had seen the P.T.L. program on television, and it had ministered to me. So even though I had never been to Heritage USA., I decided to visit. I attended the morning service and the evening service and then went directly to the Upper Room to get my life in order. The next day, I applied for a position in the Personnel Office.

A few months later they called me, and I moved down. Before going to work in the Medical school, I had been an educator, so they hired me as Director of the Tender Loving Care Adoption Agency. At that point, I was ready to do whatever the Lord wanted me to do, although I knew absolutely nothing about adoption. There was one young lady there, however, who was willing to teach me the things I needed to know. And soon afterwards I was made director of the Girl's Home.

The Girl's Home program was probably the best in the country for a maternity home. Our children are all over the country today. The first child placed for adoption now lives in Virginia Beach. He is eleven, and the family now has three more adopted children.

I remember one birth mother was only fourteen years old. She was extremely angry about the whole situation. All I could do was listen to her and try to help her. She decided to give her baby up for adoption. Years later, she called me after she had married, had other children and become a Social Worker. "Jean, you won't believe this fourteen-year-old I'm dealing with ...," she said. "She's so hard to work with!"

"Tell me about it!" I said, laughing. Now she has her Masters degree and is going into law.

Another older couple came in looking specifically for an East Indian child, and at that very moment, we had a bi-racial East Indian child whom we were having trouble placing. These are just some of the miracles.

When I left P.T.L., I started Christian Family Services Adoption Agency in our home in Tiga Cay. Now we have two offices and have placed 198 babies, all stemming from the beginnings at P.T.L. Today we continue those ministries to birth parents and adoptive parents through our agency, but they were birthed at Heritage.

I met my husband Ray at Heritage. He played the piano in the hotel, and when we were married, we had all the girls and all the foster parents at our wedding. They were, and still are, like our daughters. Several of the adoptive mothers have started support groups in their areas. So it goes on and on. Last year, we helped over 167 birth mothers. We are a 24 hour a day ministry which tries to help the parents in crisis as well as the young women and adoptive parents.

Jean Veckruise

Ann Ippolito and Jean Veckruise

Jean Veckruise in Front of Bulletin Board Holding Pictures of Babies

Dear Reader,

After watching P.T.L. on television, My husband and I decided to come down and camp. Later in 1984, when his company was transferred to South Carolina, we moved down. Since I had a great love for babies and had worked as a volunteer for Birthright, I filled out an application for us to become foster parents. After that I received three confirmations that was where God wanted me to be.

We fostered eleven babies while at P.T.L. and have fostered forty-eight since beginning to work with Jean at Christian Family Services. At P.T.L. we took all the babies to the Upper Room to have them anointed and pray that they would grow up to serve the Lord. Today we dedicate the babies and their new parents in a very touching dedication service led by Ray Veckruise.

Ann Ippolito

The next letter is from Dianne Park, wife of Jeff Park. She and Jeff were involved with the very beginnings of the Girls Home and Foster Parenting.

Dear Reader,

When Jeff and I were offered positions to move from Charlottesville to P.T.L. at Charlotte, our children were five and six. Right after we came here, Jeff started the prison ministry and going into the local jails. P.T.L. also started planning a girls home, but by that time, we had already gotten involved in helping girls in crisis pregnancies. We started getting a lot of calls from girls.

One, who already had two children and had had several abortions, came to live with us. She stayed with us until after the baby was born and she was able to go back home. Right after that, the home opened. We had great volunteers in the Girls home. When it first opened the house parents who had been chosen were not able to come right away, so our family lived there for several weeks. It was a great experience being there with the girls, forming relationships with them. Our family went over once a week after that to have dinner with the girls.

Our roles kind of changed after that. We became foster parents. That is a calling like anything else, and a calling we felt blessed to have been able to take a part in.

Dianne Park

Mark 10:43-44 says, "...*whosoever will be great among you, shall be your minister: And whosoever of you will be the chiefest, shall be servant of all. For even the son of man came not to be ministered unto, but to minister, and to give his life a ransome for many.*" Many who came to P.T.L. for a vacation or a simple desire to see the place eventually came to live on the grounds and volunteer because of the sheer enjoyment they found in the presence of the Lord and Christian friends. The volunteers that we read about in Chapter Ten were indeed *MAGNIFICENT MINERS*.

Letters from two very important "volunteers" follow. The first is from Michael Miller, best friend to Margia and me. This lady has more courage than most people I have met in my life. She has had her difficult moments concerning health, but she is always in good spirits. She never complains and is always ready to give of herself to help someone else. Michael was an usher and one of the finest. She always had the guests' welfare in mind.

Dear Reader,

I grew up in a Catholic household. We were not taught to read the Bible and I never really knew that one could have a direct line to the Lord. When I came to P.T.L., I was working as a private duty nurse. Another nurse with whom I was working, asked me if I'd like to visit P.T.L. with her. "Well, I don't know," I said. "What is it?"

"It's kind of like a religious resort," she said. I didn't want to come, but she kept begging me. So I finally told her I would if she'd find someone to substitute for me on my job. She did, so I agreed to go down with her for three days. We rented a car and stayed over by the lake.

It was a beautiful place, but I didn't understand all that was going on. The first night, we went to Camp Meeting, and I was amazed at how excited everyone was, raising their hands and crying. "Why are they doing that?" I asked my friend.

"They're giving thanks to the Lord," she told me. I wanted to ask her more questions, but she told me to wait until after the service. Later we talked further about Christianity and spiritual matters. I asked how she knew some of the things she was telling me, and she told me that she read it in the Bible. I didn't understand, because I'd never been used to reading the Bible.

Several weeks later, we managed to arrange work so we could come down again. This time we went to all the television programs and services. I had never seen the kind of response to religion that I was seeing at P.T.L. There was something that drew me to it like a magnet. On the third day, after the meeting that night, I stood alone on the edge of the lake, and said, "Dear God, I want to come here and get to know You better. But you know I've never had to do a thing in my life. I was raised with someone doing everything for me. How would I come down here to live?"

That was the beginning of my talks with the Lord. Before that, I didn't know that you could just talk to God like a person. I went back home and packed, somehow convinced that God was going to bring me to P.T.L. to live. It wasn't long until I had 32 boxes of belongings packed and sitting in my kitchen. None of them were labeled, so I didn't know where anything was and had to search all the boxes if I needed something.

I called the people at P.T.L. and asked them how I would go about buying a house there. Thus began the process of buying a home and waiting for it to be built. I quit my job in nursing and stayed home to wait for my house to be ready. At one point, I went down with a friend to find the place where my house was supposed to be built, but there weren't even any roads yet, and it was next to impossible to even find the lot. I went down again with my son, who was very shocked that I was planning to do this on my own. He couldn't believe that I had sold my house and didn't even know exactly where it was going to be built. But I trusted God, and eventually the house was built and I moved in.

I spent Thanksgiving and Christmas in my new home and then began to volunteer as an usher. I met people while I was ushering who still remember me fourteen years later. Part of my duties were to keep things quiet in the audience so as not to disturb the program or get in the way of the cameras. One day, a young man named Brent and his family came to the program. Brent was handicapped, and I tried to seat them in a place where it would not be too noticeable if he had to be excused. As it turned out, that was exactly what happened. I managed to help his mother "quietly" remove him from the auditorium and to the bathroom. We talked afterward, exchanged names, and became quite good friends. We wrote letters and spoke on the phone often. Once they even sent me a round trip ticket to come and visit them, but I couldn't go because of health problems. Brent went to the altar when he heard that and asked for prayer for me because I was sick.

I learned many things after coming here about God and friends and love. I soon found there were opportunities to witness everywhere, even when I visited the Laundromat. I thank God for the opportunity to come to P.T.L. in those early days and for the privilege of living on the grounds with my Christian friends today.

Michael Miller

The next letter is from Mary Lou Edwards who worked as Director of the Presidential Suite ministering to the guests. Through her gifts of time and talents, Mary Lou was certainly one of God's Greats!

Dear Reader,

I was born and raised in the beautiful mountains of Deep Creek Lake, Maryland. Church was a way of life in our rural community and I can't remember when I was not a Christian.

I graduated from Stayers Business College in Washington D.C. and became a construction news reporter for Dodge Reports covering the Capitol, White House, Penta-

gon, and all other government agencies and working closely with Lyndon Johnson's office.

In 1950 I married and had five wonderful children. After 32 years of marriage, our marriage broke up. We lost everything, but God answered my prayers in unique ways. There was no mistaking it was God. I'd need a certain amount of money desperately and after much prayer, I would go to pick up my mail and the exact amount of money I needed would be there in a check. This happened three times.

During all the problems, I fell apart and was admitted to Brooklane Psychiatric Hospital in Hagerstown. During that time, I reconnected with God and turned everything over to Him. Later, I attended P.T.L. with friends, Bea and Os Mason. I had never been exposed to this kind of worship but when Joel and LaBreesca Hemphill came over to pray for me, it was like God poured warm oil inside and outside of me. Such a peace came over me. I knew my circumstances hadn't changed, but I had the certainty that God would see me through the rough times ahead.

Three years later, I moved to P.T.L. and volunteered full time for seven months. Later I was appointed Director of the Presidential Lounge located on the third floor of the Heritage Grand Hotel. It was a lovely place to come to relax, read, spend time with the Lord or just have a cookie and a cup of tea or coffee. Every morning at 9:00 we had devotions. Later we opened the lounge to all partners and there were usually about 75 in attendance. Souls were saved, lives changed and folks were delivered from all sorts of curses through the teaching of our dear pastors and lay leaders. My staff of volunteers were so devoted to making each visitor feel very special. Don Edwards and I were married in the Chapel By The Lake on January 11, 1992 with Pastor Lowell Cannon officiating. We have had many trials in our five and a half years together but our God is an awesome God and He has seen us through. We feel so blessed to live on these hallowed grounds, surrounded by wonderful Christian friends. Thank you all for being a part of our lives and may God richly bless you.

Mary Lou Edwards

Volunteers at Christmas Time

One of Volunteers — Dixie Howell and Mary Lou Edwards

Chapter Eleven has told us about the other ministries of P.T.L., the *FABULOUS FINDS*. Matthew 7:7 says, *"Ask and it shall be given you; seek, and ye shall find; knock, and it shall be opened unto you."* In an interview with Rebecca Martin and Yvonne Clark, we found how God has reached out and brought the amphitheatre to life once more. These two ladies, through Narroway Productions, have followed God's calling to come to Fort Mill, South Carolina and produce a drama which is drawing crowds from near and far.

God could never have put together two more different people -- or two more perfect people for the job He had for them to do. He brought them together in college as roommates and led them into a ministry of music to youth. For years, they were satisfied that they were where they should be, doing what they should be doing, but then God began touching both of them, preparing them for what lay ahead. Eventually he led them to Fort Mill and the old amphitheatre which by that time had been closed for several years. Parts of the building were falling in. Trees had grown up in the court yard. Vandals and time had taken their toil, but these two ladies saw the potential of the place through God's eyes. With the help of numerous people, they have enabled the old amphitheater to bring the majesty of music, the thrill of drama, and the power of the gospel to the people once again.

Their 1998 season will include two productions," Two Thieves And A Savior" and "The Deliverer."

TWO THIEVES AND A SAVIOR

On His right, one who shamed Him.
On His left, one ashamed.
On His right, one who held to this life.
On His left, one who believed in a better one.
On His right, one who thought Jesus had failed.
On His left, one who knew he had failed Jesus.
In the Center
One Whose presence always calls for a decision.
Where Do you stand?
On His right? Or On His left?

THE DELIVERER

Two babies are born outside Jerusalem.
Both are born to Jewish families
Both are little boys.
Both live and die by one life-driving force.
To deliver their people.
One seeks to deliver by the sword,
The other by love.
One is called Jesus Barabbas,
The other, Jesus the Christ.
But only one will become
"The Deliverer"

These two epic musicals will be presented live in the beautiful, biblical outdoor amphitheater, King's Arena, from June 12 - August 29, 1998 at 8:30 P.M. and September 4 - October 24, 1998, at 7:30 P.M. on Fridays and Saturdays. The two shows will alternate weekends. For more information you can contact NarroWay Productions, 9700 Regent Parkway, Box 106, Fort Mill, S.C., 29715 (803-802-2300). Join them this year for the live animals, authentic biblical staging, beautiful costumes, exciting cast and choir, in these entertaining and powerful stories.

The next letter is from the Driver family and tells how much the Passion Play meant to them and what an impression it made on their grandson.

Dear Reader,
We have come every year since the conception of P.T.L. The fellowship, the sweet spirit, the fact that there were no denominational labels drew us here. We came from a more conservative church, but we found the openness here to be wonderful. Once we brought all of our family down and went to the Passion Play. Our four year old grandson, Brian went back and ran to his daddy who had not been able to come with us. "Daddy, Daddy," he said, "I know Jesus is still alive." It was so precious to see children like Brian

come to know the Lord at such an early age because of the influence of P.T.L. And the spirit is still here with the Time Share owners.

Margaurite and Harold Driver

Chapter Twelve has told us about the *PRICELESS PROMISES* from God that people found through the workshops, seminars, and musicians at P.T.L. Galatians 6:1 says, *"Brethren, if a man be overtaken in a fault, ye which are spiritual, restore such an one in the spirit of meekness; considering thyself, lest thou also be tempted."* The workshops and seminars were there to teach and train, to revitalize and restore. God reminds us in John 8:32 *"... And ye shall know the truth and the truth shall make you free."* This is the secret of freedom from sin, sickness, and all the curses of this life. Christ died to set men free. Many who found freedom at the workshops and seminars hastened to the Upper Room close by to pray and receive God in a fuller extent. I pray that those who attended the workshops and seminars and heard the beautiful music will carry on today in the face of the onslaught of Satan.

Following are some letters that show you some of the jewels that were mined at P.T.L. workshops and seminars:

Dear Reader,

After living life in an ignorant state about the things that plagued my family, I discovered at a Healing Seminar in the Grand Hotel at P.T.L. that God had bigger and better things for me.

Beginning at age three, when the "reality" of "life" was forced upon me, everything went from bad to worse. I guess it was what is called today a dysfunctional family. My parents had no church upbringing and lived themselves in a state of confusion and misery.

In the Healing Seminar we were able to express our hatred, anger, frustrations and general discontent with our respective situations. We learned to fight back when Satan tries to throw our past back in our faces in order to keep us down.

I was able to deal with the task of forgiving my parents

for not knowing that things in our lives were wrong and not being able to correct them through Jesus Christ.

I finally realized how their lives must have been up to the very day they died. Dad in 1983 and Mom in 1984.

I began to learn how to take responsibility for my own life and practice breaking the curse over my own three children.

Praise God for P.T.L. and the people who devoted themselves to helping others "overcome."

Sandra Jones

Dear Reader,

In 1981, my wife Loisann was struggling with a possible reoccurrence of cancer when we first came to P.T.L. accompanied by her son, Darren, age 14. We spent the night at a nearby motel because no accommodations were available at P.T.L. Next day, during the morning service, we discovered Gary Greenawalt of Eagles Nest in California would be speaking in the evening service, the "Camp Meeting" on the subject of "Back Masking."

Darren, his 17-year-old sister, Debbie, and their youth group at Bethel United Methodist Church in Wooster, Ohio (where I was pastor for ten years) had been studying his tapes on the subject. Darren had written a paper on the subject and presented it to his high school class.

Darren was so enthused about hearing Gary in person that he spent 3 ½ hours sitting and standing at the door of "The Barn" so he could be first in line and be able to get a front seat for the service.

When we saw his enthusiasm and the other fun and fellowship he enjoyed here, we bought our first timeshare unit and came back for a full week. Though his mother went to be with the Lord in 1984, Darren went on to finish high school, graduate from Rhema in 1986, and is now Associate Pastor at New Covenant Fellowship in Columbia, S.C.

Darren's sister, Debbie, and her husband Wendell Miller, also went to Rhema. Wendell graduated in 1985, and he and Debbie both came to work at P.T.L. full time. My wife, Sandra, and I were married at P.T.L., January 6,

1986 by Pastor Larry Soles of the Shield of Faith Church in Rock Hill, S.C. and have celebrated our anniversary every year since then here at our Timeshare at P.T.L.

Doug Jones

Dear Reader,

My involvement with P.T.L. began when I started watching the television programs . One day they were advertising a Personal Growth Workshop, and I had been wanting to attend an Inner Healing Workshop, but I felt like the Lord was telling me to go to this Personal Growth Workshop for some reason. So I made arrangements to go.

As soon as I came on the ground, I could feel the presence of the Lord. In the workshop, we were all sitting around in circles of about ten people each. For some reason, I couldn't explain, I began to weep. One of the counselors came over to me. I had been trying to deal with the death of my husband. And come to find out as we went around the group, most of the people had lost a loved one, a child or a spouse or a parent. After that, they changed the whole workshop from Personal Growth to Inner Healing.

I thought it was very interesting that God would send me down here to a workshop I hadn't planned on attending and then change the subject of the workshop to deal with my problems. It had to have been of the Lord for the theme of the workshop to have changed.

I came from "a not so good area" in Detroit, and each time I'd come down to P.T.L., I would literally cry when I had to leave. The last time I vacationed in 1985, I was driving home and praying in my heart about what to do. After that, the Lord moved us down in two weeks, and we've been here ever since.

Teresa Harper

Dear Reader,

We have lived on the grounds of what was known as P.T.L. for twelve years. Back in Wichita, Kansas, I watched P.T.L. on television long before, Charles, my husband, would even sit down and listen. The program was very special to me. I began to want to move there and committed everything to God to work it out.

God began to change Charles' heart for the program and then to move in unexpected ways. One day Roe Messner called and wanted Charles to fly with him over to look at P.T.L. He was looking for an electrical superintendent to supervise a large crew of men. Charles felt that it would be too hard for him at his age, but surprisingly Charles did consent to take the job. He found us an apartment on the grounds (when we were told there were 4500 people on the waiting list for housing). We felt God was opening doors for the final move.

I had second thoughts as our son, Troy, and I prepared to leave family and friends of many years. The Christmas lights were on when Troy and I pulled up in the big rental truck carrying every possession we had. It was an awesome sight. I met neighbors immediately. They even helped move us in.

It was a true blessing to be able to go hear all the different preachers and speakers. We had the privilege of seeing Main Street put together. There was a constant excitement in the air. People prayed with one another and helped to carry their burdens anyway they could. Many types of people from all walks of life seemed to hear the call. People spent hours at the Upper Room praying, taking communion and hearing the Word of God preached. There was a staff of pastors to minister to the needs of the people, and Sunday morning services were so crowded, one could hardly find a seat.

The Bible Seminars were unsurpassed. They had the finest speakers and musicians that could be found. Shirley Dougan headed them, and she was extremely talented. Every Bible Seminar was packed, and the participants came out blessed.

People's lives were touched in many ways. It was a place where God was a refuge and peace could be found.

I began conducting seminars and working in the women's ministry. I was able to offer seminars that I felt the Lord had blessed me with to share with others. I put my heart and soul into sharing with all the many people. My "Looking Good" seminars were well received by the crowds and offers came to travel to churches to share outside of P.T.L. It was a blessing I will never forget.

Susan Bankston

The next letter is from Charles and Joyce Loose, a fine couple who live on the grounds today, and who found hope and release in the workshops at P.T.L.

Dear Reader,

Charles and I came to P.T.L. searching for help. I needed help personally because I had been rejected all my life as a child and my eighteen year marriage had failed. After that I fell into a deep depression. But after watching the P.T.L. Club on television, I saw there was hope.

We went through a really difficult time with Charles alcohol problem, but after he was delivered from alcohol, we came to P.T.L. and found a love and unity among the people we'd never seen before. We became partners and came four times a year. What we received in help and through the seminars and workshops could never be paid for in dollars and cents. We went to marriage workshops, the inner healing workshops, the Christian Counseling Training.

The workshops were the best in the world. We have seen people set free. God is faithful. He can touch anyone. Even after P.T.L. closed down, we kept coming. If no one else loves you, we found that Jesus will love you and he will bring people into your life who will love you.

Charles and Joyce Loose

Judy Chevez was the strength behind the deep teachings at the P.T.L. Seminars. She is known all over the world in Christian circles, and those of us sit under her Bible studies and preaching today recognize the sparkling diamonds which are present in her teachings. God blesses Judy, and God is blessed through Judy. I hope someday she will tell her complete story so it can continue to benefit thousands of people long after she is gone in the same way she has helped people throughout her life.

Dear Reader,

I was born in Albuquerque, New Mexico, in 1923. On my 16th birthday I went to Los Angeles to live with my married sister and got a job. Eventually my parents and family came to L.A. too. At age nineteen, I was saved, and the Lord called me to preach the gospel almost immediately afterward. I enrolled in Bible college and graduated in 1946 and went out into the evangelistic field where I've been ever since.

I never married by choice. I wanted to be unencumbered so I could be under his command totally. In 1973, I came to P.T.L. in California. I hadn't even heard of P.T.L. until my secretary, Fern, told me about the new ministry which had just come to southern California. "It is wonderful," she said, "something old-timey, like we were used to..."

So when I got back to California, I sat down to watch the program on television. I was very blessed at what I heard and felt from the telecast. Later, Fern said she heard the spirit of the Lord speaking to her. "Before this week is over, Judy is going to Santa Ana from door to door..." This was on Monday, and she didn't tell me about it until Wednesday.

When the Lord speaks to us, it has never failed to come to pass as He said. I thought to myself, it is the hottest month of the year, and the only thing I could think of was I'd be going door to door handing out tracts, and I didn't particularly look forward to it.

On Friday, we went to visit our friend Paul and his wife Jo. He had been asked by P.T.L. to be interviewed, but he called and asked my advice. He told me he was so busy that he didn't have time and he didn't need the exposure. I told him he needed to go. It ended up with Paul and Jo inviting Fern and me to go with them.

When we got to the studio, we met Jim, and I was introduced as an evangelist. When the telecast started, Fern and I sat in the audience and watched the interview for the first hour. When Paul and Jo came down, Fern and I got up to leave, but the Program Director told us that Jim wanted to interview us.

I shared some of the tremendous answers to prayer and told about some of the meetings we had been conducting up to that time. I told them what God had done for me and what He was able to do for anyone. The phones began to ring. People began to make pledges of money to help with the ministry, and the owner of the television station called and told us to stay on the air. We were there until after 2:00 in the morning.

Jim asked me on camera to join their staff. And that was the beginning of how we came into P.T.L. After the telecast was over, Fern and I walked out to the parking lot. "Fern," I said, "do you realize where we are? We're in Santa Ana!" We had not realized until that moment that we were in Santa Ana and that I had been going house to house over television. We came to that ministry, led of the Lord, never asking, never soliciting.

I have never, in almost fifty years of ministering, sent out a card or made a phone call to ask for an opportunity to preach or share. Years ago, the spirit of the Lord told me, "As Israel of old, when I led them through that vast wilderness, so will I lead you. I will lead you in paths you know not of. And as I led them forth, I will lead you likewise."

I never ask a pastor about the size of his congregation or the fee. I always tell them I will come on a love offering basis, once a week. At one international convention, this black sister came to me. "I pastor a church in Los Vegas, Nevada," she said, "and we'd like to have you for a revival. But I must tell you about my little church. There are only three in my congregation. I have a 16-year-old teenage Mexican girl, a black elder, and myself. Our offerings are anywhere from seventy-five cents to $1.50."

In the natural, 99% of evangelists would have given some kind of a story why they couldn't come. But the Spirit of the Lord gave me the green signal. "Sister, when do you want us to come?" I asked. The bible says, "they that are led by the spirit of the Lord, they are the sons of God." To be led is for us to follow, not to question or to argue. So she gave us a date for the revival.

Now we had a house payment, but that was God's business. We had a car payment, but that was my Father's business. We had bills like everyone else. We live in a commercial world, but we packed and went.

The Bible tells us, "My father who seeth in secret, he will reward you openly." I have practiced that verse all the years in serving the Lord. I have never asked for a certain amount, even though I needed it. But that was only for my Father's ears. We were there for three weeks, and the spirit of the Lord spoke to the woman who had physically built that church many years back, Viola Dale. She was living in Fairbanks, Alaska, but the Spirit of the Lord spoke to her and told her to come down to Los Vegas. She obeyed, and when she got there the revival was in progress. She preached. The pastor preached. I preached and the church was so full the children had to sit on the floor. We were simply preaching the pureness of His word. People were coming to Christ and bodies were being healed. People gave and gave. God supplied that church and when we left, they had money in the bank and all our needs were taken care of.

I could tell you all day and all night, the goodness and the love and the grace of the almighty God for all those who trust in him. I have even been invited to the White House when Reagan was President. They didn't know me, but "the Lord knoweth them that are His." When the Lord opens a door, --- "Behold I set an open door before you that no man can shut," we need to go through that door. So I met with the president, other outstanding people in government, and other women evangelists and ministers. They had invited us to come because they thought we had an influence with the nation. When the President gave us an opportunity to speak, I told him, "If this nation would operate on the Word of God, we would be most blessed."

When I came to Heritage, I was still living in my home in Long Beach. Jim had invited me to come down several times, but I felt like I needed to stay where I was. Then one day I felt like God was calling me there, so I agreed to come down as a staff counselor. My secretary, Fern, came down, and now we've been here 22 years.

Since I was a staff counselor, everyone would come to me with their problems. The first time I was on television, calls came from pastors wanting me to conduct revivals. So I was going out and leading revivals at night and during the day I was counseling with the P.T.L. staff. I have never worked anywhere in my life with such wonderful staff members. They were the cream of the crop, and they are all still in ministry today, either their own, or on other ministry teams. What happened here influenced what happened to many, many people afterward.

Jim asked me to start teaching seminars. I taught the first seminar and 250 seminars after that. I also taught the last seminar at P.T.L. So many people would come to the seminars that the ball room would be filled. There were 6 million people that came to P.T.L. that last year. It was the third most visited park in the United States.

We must remember that the Lord knows us. He is maturing his people, getting them ready for a tremendous moving of God. God never uses novices in the greater works. He uses mature, seasoned saints and that's what we're here for -- seasoning the Church of the Lord Jesus Christ, getting them ready for Him.

For the last six years, I have been leading services at Aunt Susan Harrison's home under the mandate of the Lord. I have stopped traveling now. Before that I traveled to Mexico, the islands, Newfoundland, Canada, and all over the United States ministering the gospel.

We don't have a membership at the meetings at Aunt Susan's house. We never ask for an offering. There is a little basket where people put in whatever they feel led to. I am still trying simply to follow the will of the Lord for my life.

Judy Chevez

Two very sparkling diamonds of P.T.L. were Bob and Jeannie Johnson. In the following letter, Bob tells some of the reasons they came "and stayed" with P.T.L. They were not only jewels themselves, but they discovered jewels all around them.

Dear Reader,

Before coming to P.T.L., I managed a jewelry store. My wife, Jeanne, and I came to P.T.L. because we thought the ministry was a great avenue to reach people. And from reports that we hear all over the country, the P.T.L. ministry did reach a lot of lives and touch many people. It made a difference in people's lives.

We enjoyed our years in serving the Lord through the music ministry of P.T.L. We made some very good friends. One special individual was the young girl, Brooke Roberts, whom we met at one of the dinner theater productions. Jeanne and I were walking through the audience singing when I looked down and saw this little blond girl looking up at me. I reached down, picked her up, and held her in my arms while we were singing. It was an instant love between her, Jeannie, and myself. That love is still there. I don't think it will ever end.

She has been such a great inspiration to us down through the years. She is in high school now, not the little girl that I could reach down and pick up any more, but she is still singing. We love her and her whole family dearly. Her grandparents are great people.

Our lives were enriched by meeting Brooke and her family and many, many other special people at P.T.L. We only hope that we enriched the lives of others in a similar way. Today we continue to minister with music, traveling all over the country. And I would say to you that the most important thing we can do is to keep our eyes on the Lord. He is our source. God will never fail us. If we keep our eyes on Him, we're going to be all right no matter what happens.

Bob Johnson

RARE RICHES were, and are today, found in the residents, visitors and special friends of P.T.L. We heard from many of them in Chapter Thirteen. Matthew 9:37-38 tells us, *"The harvest truly is plenteous, but the laborers are few; pray ye therefore the Lord of the harvest that he will send forth laborers into his harvest."* One of God's laborers is Gretchen Mack. I have known Gretchen for many years and her dedication to the Lord and the health of His people is outstanding. Her whole life has been committed to serving God and helping other people be in good health.

Dear Reader,

I came to P.T.L. because the Lord sent me here after my husband passed away. I opened a Nutrition Center on Main Street, and I remember looking out the front many times and seeing so many people on Main Street that there was barely room to walk.. Many of the people who came to the Nutrition Center have maintained a healthy body since that time, but the most wonderful part about having a store on Main Street was the opportunities to share and pray together.

Through the wonderful workshops, people received healing of the spirit and the mind. We know this place belongs to God. One night a young man broke into my home and attacked me. He was looking for money to buy cocaine. I had been working on the phones, and while the attack was occurring, the woman in charge of the phones felt like God was telling her to pray for one of her counselors. As she and the others prayed, the young man became afraid and ran out the back door. God's answer was immediate.

After the young man was arrested, I asked Jeff Park and the prison ministry to call on him, and I believe that he has accepted the Lord. God is so good, and I still feel totally safe in my home. I believe there was a reason for that happening. I believe it was to show that God still loved me and that he saved my life through those counselors who were praying for me even though they didn't know for whom they were praying. God knew and God knew that He still wanted me to be helping other people.

Gretchen Mack

The next letter is from Pastor Sam Johnson:

Dear Reader,
While I was at P.T.L., I worked with the missions, home and overseas, and after P.T.L. closed, I was asked to pastor a church for two years. But then I went back into missions for another four years. I think people came to P.T.L. because people here cared about them. The television program, of course, was what helped built P.T.L. to what it was. Jesus said, I will build my church and the gates of hell shall not prevail against it. And here we are, ten years later, and the church marches on. God's will marches on, bigger and better than ever. It's not because of man, an organization, a denomination. It's because of Christ.
Today I am helping raise support to build an orphanage and a Bible School in Romania. In the last four years I've concentrated on missions in Eastern Europe. Basically I have given my energies to the country of Romania.
Pastor Sam Johnson

The next letter is from a man who is devoted to serving God, Michael Lint.

Dear Reader,
It is most important for us to recognize when we're wanting to do something ourself or when we're being called of God. There are a lot of turning points in life that you have to go through before many of those things happen. You must go through periods of growth, development and transition. Before coming to P.T.L. I was going through all kinds of developments in my life.
The most important was when I was in the third grade and accepted Jesus Christ into my life. Everything that I did from that point on could only go so far. Even though I made a lot of mistakes, there were limits. After high school, I wanted to go to a place that was centered on Jesus, so I went to Oral Roberts University. Later I went to work for

Trinity Broadcasting, C.B.N., and ended up at P.T.L. What God was doing through me during those periods, what he was working in and out of me during that time is what is important. I know that I came to P.T.L. as a direct command from God. When your ears are attentive to His word, you become accustomed to His voice. It is not a loud voice, but it is so powerful that it just burns within you. So I tried to listen during that stage of growth for me. God was in control of the whole picture, no matter what was going on in my life, or what went on at P.T.L or didn't go on at P.T.L. God was still in control. You'll gain far more than you'll ever lose if you let everything be entirely up to the Lord. There are absolutely incredible benefits that follow obedience. Some materially, but more spiritually. You come to see things that you have never seen before.

I believe that the moment we accept Jesus Christ, the Holy Spirit comes within us to reside. No matter how far we go in the Lord, or how long we've been in the church, each and every day, our hearts and minds are being continually cleansed from the dirt and grime of the world. It's an ongoing process.

People came here, weary of their lives, and returned home with joy, the darkness gone from their eyes. They had a clear vision of the spiritual truths of God they'd never seen before. There was that kind of freedom here.

Let God move in your life. There is no magical formula or rules and regulations to which you have to abide. If the Holy Spirit has taken up residence inside you, you'll know. When I came here from C.B.N., I bought a condo and started a prayer ministry in my home.

Michael Lint

This letter is from a couple who have truly seen God's touch in their lives, James and Betty Lentz:

Dear Reader,
We live in Lancaster, Pennsylvania. On August 25, 1985, Betty went to the doctor for an examination. She had felt that something wasn't right. They put her through a series of x-rays and tests, and three days later she had surgery. Before she was out of surgery, they told me that she had ovarian cancer and only a few months to live.

I called down to Heritage and the Gideon ministry to ask for prayer. She was in the hospital two weeks, and then started chemo treatments. We got to the point where we thought we were at the end. Betty was put in isolation. Then she told me about an experience she had had in which she talked to The Great Physician. "I just wanted to talk to someone who knew what I was going through," She said. "Someone who would understand." He told me, "you can tell me anything and everything." So I started going down the list of problems and complaints. I tried to tell him all the things I had suffered, and how tired I was. He told me to lie there and rest for a while. I fell asleep and slept three hours, and when I woke up He told me I had been talking to the Great Physician. He said, "I am the healer of all your infirminities." I listened, and I heard Him say the same thing three times. I thought of when the Lord spoke to Samuel the third time, so I answered, "Yes Lord, I know that you are the Great Physician."

The next day, she had added strength and slept well that night. She was even better the next day and night. On the next day, Thanksgiving morning, she said she felt a clean feeling come over her whole body, like she had been washed. She and I agreed together in prayer before her exploratory surgery that they would find no cancer. And that is exactly what happened. They could find no signs of cancer.

P.T.L. taught us that you can make it, you're on the verge of a miracle, don't give up. We had their signs posted all around us. And we felt their prayers during the whole experience.
James and Betty Lentz

Another exciting letter comes from Gene and Evie Eddie and tells about their experiences of finding treasures at P.T.L.

Dear Reader,
We came to P.T.L. from Morgantown, West Virginia, where we had a plumbing/heating/cooling business. We had seen the P.T.L. Program on television, so we decided to come by and visit Heritage on our way back home from Morehead City. After seeing it, we knew we wanted to retire here. You could feel the anointing when you first came on the grounds.

I worked at the switchboard in the hotel for a while and got to know a lot of people. I had to leave the job after about ten months because we were looking for a house. Gene worked in maintenance on the grounds. It was a good place to be. Anything we gave was a gift to God, and we have no regrets. God has honored that with many, many good memories. He has done so many wonderful things in our lives. He has healed me, saved my life through numerous health problems and illness, and brought me through safely.
Gene and Eva Eddie

The next letter is from Phil Darling and is a letter from one partner to another:

Dear Reader,
I think of one summer when our two young granddaughters stayed with us. I see them on the carousel, riding the train, driving the antique cars and with thousands of others enjoying the incomparable Heritage Island. There was a never ceasing movement of kids of all ages; walking, laughing, swimming, eating, or just sitting and looking. There is a constant flow of orange and blue tubes up the hill carried by exhilarated youngsters on their way for trip after trip down several slides. Some revel in the big wave pool, and others relax listening to gospel music.

I remember our going to the Passion Play -- such a blessing and victory at the resurrection. We went to the Upper Room for communion with the two little girls. I thank God for Pastor Don Duncan and his explanation of the meaning of communion. Those two little girls will never forget it. They will also never forget the July 4th parade, or the entertainment at Buffalo Park, or the fireworks.

This truly was a place for all the family of God to come and commune with each other. We gloried in the greatness of God, as when Mike Adkins introduced his anointed song "Adoration" to the television audience, and the camera crews were weeping. I think of the time Elsa and I came out of the Upper Room and found a little girl on the "walk of faith" going from one scripture verse to another praying and crying in despair. We were able to offer our concern and comfort her, a sister in the family of God. We met a 73-year-old widow in the lobby of the Grand Hotel two days after it opened. She was alone, grieving over the recent loss of her husband and son. Because of the partner center, we were there to be with her on Christmas Eve and Christmas Day. She went home much better, because she knew someone cared.

I could go on telling about the dream of Heritage USA.-- the dream that came alive and still lives today in those who came to P.T.L. Let us forgive and get on with it. To God be the glory!

Phil Darling

The following letter is from Ann Kintner from Cincinnati, Ohio, and tells of her first and subsequent trips to P.T.L. and of the diamonds she found.

Dear Reader,

My husband Keith and I, along with some good friends, decided to go to Heritage USA for Christmas. I clearly recall driving through the gate and down the boulevard where the flags of the nations were on poles along the road. Only there were no flags. Each pole had become a Christmas tree, with multi-strings of lights stretched out form the top to a circle on the ground to form a tree. The road curved ahead and the trees formed a dramatic row as far as the eye could see.

None of the other details of the trip matter any longer except the evening we spent walking around the grounds. The mood was made complete by the carols which filled the air. The real world wasn't real. I was lifted into a different realm. My spirit soured. It was a celebration of the birth of my Savior!

A number of the P.T.L. staff became close friends, particularly Dick and June Hall and Michael Miller. Such special people. We have been to Heritage every year since, even after Hugo came. Evergreens were at a 45 degree angle. Huge trees were down, much wreckage was apparent. The Grand Hotel stood idle and somewhat damaged. Sad? Yes, sad. But as I took daily walks around the fallen trees and through the woods and recreation areas that I had come to know so well, I prayed. I thanked God for all the good that had happened there and asked His forgiveness for the sin that had occurred. Then I prayed for God to forgive "this place" and restore it according to His will. I am "knit" to this place. Keith and I attend the Heritage Reunions each Labor Day weekend. If by chance your heart was also "knit" to this place, come and join us this year!

Ann Kintner

I would like to close out this section with a letter from Myra Bumgardner telling her views on what has happened in and through P.T.L. She so adequately speaks for all of us in these days, letting her words shine like a beacon to bring those who have been hurt to the healing power of Jesus.

Dear Reader,

Tabloids! Articles! Books! Talk Shows! The grasping and the greedy have milked the P.T.L. story year after year. Feeding the base curiosity of man, the media has had a field day. The world and the church alike, have dined on this particular scandal with a seemingly insatiable appetite -- devouring and savoring every evil report.

Yet -- with all the reporting, the real story of P.T.L. has never been told. The Jim and Tammy Story is not the P.T.L. story. The heart of P.T.L. pulsated from the constant going and coming of the masses. It's heartbeat was the hurting, the wounded, and the lame who came seeking not man, but God. These were not disappointed.

The real story of P.T.L. rests in the hearts and lives of such people. People whom the press would not consider newsworthy and whom the world at large would show little interest in. It rests in the hearts of those who shine, today, as a light in a very dark world whose flames were kindled on the grounds of Heritage U.S.A.

Myra Bumgardner

Chapter Fifteen

TOMORROW'S TREASURES

Ray's Closing Letter

Dear Reader,
Writing and compiling this book has been one of the greatest blessings of my life. Without God, it would have been impossible, but Matthew 19:26 tells us "... with God all things are possible." I have met exciting new Christian friends, renewed old acquaintances and recaptured wonderful memories.

I am so grateful to God that thousands came to P.T.L. for whatever reason. Initially, many came to be released from pain and anguish, some with unsolved problems, loneliness, heartaches, and broken spirits. They sought relief and release, peace, and a new life. Others came simply to enjoy and experience the presence of the Lord with other Christians. Often they felt a tug on their heart strings and began to minister to those in need with an arm around their shoulders and prayers.

All discovered that their lives had been changed in some way by their visit to P.T.L. Some found a new life through Jesus. Others discovered diamonds and treasures of love for our Lord and each other. P.T.L. was a God inspired min-

istry, but as these stories and letters you have read show, -- it was not the buildings or the programs or the grounds. It was not man, but God Himself working, through those who ministered, to accomplish His purpose.

I know when you began reading this book, some of you may still have had a small chunk of criticism in your heart. We must remember, however, that we all have the root of temptation within us, and we need to deal kindly with ones who have been tempted or fallen. How can we demand that others be perfect when we ourselves are not perfect?

I hope through reading these personal letters that coal-like criticism has been transformed by God's loving hand into shimmering diamonds of understanding and love. Ephesians 1:17-19 tells us:

"That the God of our Lord Jesus Christ, the Father of glory, may give unto you the spirit of wisdom and revelation in the knowledge of him: the eyes of your understanding being enlightened; that ye may know what is the hope of his calling, and what the riches of his glory of his inheritance in the saints, and what is the exceeding greatness of his power to usward who believe, according to the working of his mighty power; in Christ Jesus."

I once heard a prayer which said, "Grant me, O God, to know what should be known; to love that which ought to be loved, to praise that which pleaseth you most, to hold up high that which is precious in your sight. Suffer me not to judge according to my eyes, nor to give sentence according to what ignorant men hear and speak; but to have true judgement between visible and spiritual things, and above all to always seek after the will of your good pleasure." I hope that will be the prayer on all of our lips as we put down this book and go out to meet the world.

This place, home to many, didn't just fall -- it changed -- from a lofty, blessed ministry to a community of Christian residence, and the people of this community still love each other. They still pray and still feel the presence of God here. They still believe that it is God's place and not man's.

Let us look closely with our magnifying glasses, dig deeper with our thoughts, and brush aside the darkness to expose the diamonds. We should drop our stones as the scribes and pharisees did in John 8 when reminded of our own sins and seek God's wisdom, being slow to condemn and quick to show compassion.

If we ask ourselves how much one soul is worth, we would all agree that one soul is worth untold treasures. Think then of the thousands of souls that were saved in response to the P.T.L. radio programs, the television broadcasts, the amphitheater drama, the workshops and seminars, the Upper Room, the prison ministry, the Girl's Home and Adoption Agency, telephone calls, and the simple acceptance and love given so freely by people like Uncle Henry, the musicians, the volunteers, visitors, residents, staff, and God's special children.

From this time on, instead of focusing on the problems at P.T.L., may we center our hearts on the glory and honor that God received through souls that were saved and lives that were changed at P.T.L. May God have mercy on us all and renew within us His Spirit of Love and forgiveness. Let's go out and do as Matthew 5:16 instructs: "LET YOUR LIGHT SO SHINE BEFORE MEN, THAT THEY MAY SEE YOUR GOOD WORKS, AND GLORIFY YOUR FATHER WHICH IS IN HEAVEN."

Your friend in Christ,
Ray Walters

TO ORDER ADDITIONAL COPIES OF "DIAMONDS IN THE ROUGH"

SEND CHECK OR MONEY ORDER FOR $15.95 PLUS $3.00 SHIPPING AND HANDLING.

TO: RAY WALTERS
423 SWEET GUM DRIVE, FORT MILL, S.C. 29715
OR CALL 803-548-7718.

* * * * *

PERHAPS YOU TOO HAVE A STORY YOU WOULD LIKE TO SHARE WITH THE AUTHOR FOR THE NEXT BOOK, IF SO, PLEASE SUBMIT TO "MORE DIAMONDS IN THE ROUGH," C/O RAY WALTERS, 423 SWEET GUM DRIVE, FORT MILL, S.C. 29715.

* * * * *

FOR EDITING, GHOST-WRITING, OR HELP WITH YOUR OWN BOOK OR WRITING PROJECT — REQUEST A BROCHURE OF AVAILABLE SERVICES FROM:
LINDA TOMBLIN
P.O. BOX 404, SPINDALE, N.C. 28160

Dear Reader,

    We have purposely left these pages blank, so that you might write your own personal prayer letter to God. May it be a plea for love and forgiveness from all of us that will completely overshadow any pain or resentment that might remain for some.

    For it is only in a spirit of love and God's grace that we will continue to link arms and hearts and march forward to many Hidden Treasures for God.

Dear God,